THE
ROWAN/BROTHER
DESIGNER MACHINE KNITTING
BOOK

STEPHEN SHEARD

CENTURY
LONDON SYDNEY AUCKLAND JOHANNESBURG

First published in 1989 by Century Hutchinson Ltd,
Brookmount House, 62–65 Chandos Place,
Covent Garden,
London WC2N 4NW

Century Hutchinson Australia Pty Ltd,
20 Alfred Street, Milsons Point,
Sydney, NSW 2061, Australia

Century Hutchinson New Zealand Ltd,
PO Box 40–086, Glenfield, Auckland 10,
New Zealand

Century Hutchinson South Africa Pty Ltd,
PO Box 337, Bergvlei, 2012 South Africa

Editor: Sue Hopper
Design: Patrick McLeavey
Photography: Tony Boase; garment detail photographs
by Edward Hill; photographs on pages 2, 21, 23, 90–91
and 92 by Eamon J McCabe
Artwork: John Hutchinson
Make-up: Anna Clare of Syncro
Stylist: Kim Hargreaves
Models: Judy Mancini, Jenny Brunt, Maxine Restall,
Amelia Bryant and Charles Pegg of Models One

Note The yarns quoted in this book are available in either
balls or skeins, many of them are also available on cones.
The quantities stated are approximate. The patterns in
this book are not to be knitted for resale.

British Library Cataloguing in Publication Data

Sheard, Stephen
    The Rowan/Brother designer machine knitting book.
    1. Machine knitting, – Patterns
    I. Title
    746.43'2041

    ISBN 0-7126-2241-1

Printed in Italy

ACKNOWLEDGEMENTS

Many thanks to Margaret Lockwood for her patience
and skill in knitting all the garments that we
photographed in the book.
Also to Sue Hopper, our editor, for all the checking
and perfecting of patterns.
Particularly, thanks to the Designer Knitters for all
their help and support over the years.
Special thanks to Penny Burton of Platform One,
Towngate, Holmfirth and Pink Cadillac, Market Walk,
Huddersfield for clothes and accessories.
Also to Hubberton Trading, Holmfirth.

CONTENTS

INTRODUCTION

Machine knitting has become very popular in recent years. The knitting machine makers, and particularly Jones Brother, have designed more and more sophisticated knitting machines to enable knitters to develop endless possibilities in colour patterns and stitch designs. Unfortunately, with a few notable exceptions, the quality of pattern designs and visual excellence have not kept pace with the machine advances. Rowan's collaboration with Jones Brother in this lavish book is an attempt to redress the balance.

Over the past few years Rowan, in partnership with some of the world's leading knitwear designers, has worked to raise the standard of knitwear design. Two major factors have made success possible. Firstly, Britain produces many of the best designers, universally acknowledged by both the stores and the press of the world. The tradition of skilled British handknitters and the high standard of our many Art Colleges have produced a steady stream of creative talent. Secondly, these designers need natural fibre, classic yarns in large colour ranges. Yarns should be used rather as an artist works with his paint palette; they must not dominate the designer's flair, but should be the basis on to which the pattern, colour, stitch texture and fashion styling are built. More and more spinners are realising the sense of using wool, cotton, silk and other luxurious, natural fibres. They are also going back to the classic yarns after a number of years of more exotic yarns, which give added value to the producer, but do not allow the knitwear designer's skill to shine through.

The handknitting designers have led the way and many, like Kaffe Fassett, Sasha Kagan, Edina Ronay and Susan Duckworth are becoming household names. Creativity apart, the secret of their success is the fact that they are the producers, working as craftsmen, close to their materials and the customer. This close contact enables them to respond quickly to fashion trends, therefore staying ahead of the market and remaining individual in their designs. To be a successful designer you have to dare to be different.

This book brings to you, for the first time, the best machineknit designers (some of whom also produce handknit collections each season). Hardly any of them work with spinners to produce pattern leaflets, partly because they are rightly protective of their hard-earned success in making beautiful garments. So why invite imitation? However, this is more than compensated for by their natural inclination to share their skills, to spread good design to a wider audience.

Without exception the knitwear designers featured in this book take design as the core of their businesses. On this they will not compromise. Design is not something that is added as an afterthought, it is the very reason for the garment's existence. So much of our craft is about technical expertise but to these designers this aspect is secondary to using their time to produce something of real beauty.

Their main aim is for you to be inspired to go on and create lots of your own designs. Throughout the book we have included a few of the designers' ideas on alternative colour combinations, which give a glimpse of how designs may be developed down many and varied paths.

JAMIE AND JESSI SEATON

PAPER CHAINS

Right: The slip stitches form the slightly textured effect on this cool cotton Fair Isle jersey.

MATERIALS
Rowan Cabled Mercerised Cotton
250 (275, 300) g/10 (11, 12) oz in white (shade 302)
50 (100, 100) g/2 (4, 4) oz in pale mauve (shade 311)
50 (100, 100) g/2 (4, 4) oz in spode blue (shade 307)
50g/2oz in blue scan (shade 306)
Rowan Sea Breeze
50 (100, 100) g/2 (4, 4) oz in polka (shade 530)
50 (100, 100) g/3 (4, 4) oz in mermaid (shade 547)
50 (100, 100) g/3 (4, 4) oz in strawberry ice (shade 546)
50 (100, 100) g/2 (4, 4) oz in true blue (shade 541)
50 (50, 100) g/2 (2, 4) oz in lilac (shade 544)
5 buttons for cardigan

MEASUREMENTS
To fit bust 91 (97, 102) cm/36 (38, 40) in
Actual size
Bust 106 (112, 118) cm/42 (44, 46½) in
Length 61 (62, 64) cm/24 (24½, 25) in
Sleeve seam 46 (47. 5, 48) cm/18 (18¾, 19) in

TENSION
30 sts and 62 rows to 10cm/4in worked over st st with TD at approx 8

MACHINE
Any Brother standard gauge electronic or punchcard machine with ribbing attachment or equivalent (If ribbing attachment not available see Alternative methods of ribbing in techniques – p.123)

PATTERN SEQUENCE FOR BACK, FRONT AND SLEEVES

ROWS	PATTERN SETTING	COLOUR IN FEEDER A	COLOUR IN FEEDER B	ROWS	PATTERN SETTING	COLOUR IN FEEDER A	COLOUR IN FEEDER B
Punchcard 1 and 2 (joined together in a circle)				51–52	Fair Isle	lilac	white
Lock card				53–56	slip	lilac	
				57–60	Fair Isle	mermaid	white
1–4	plain	white		61–64	slip	true blue	
Release card				65–66	Fair Isle	true blue	white
5–8	Fair Isle	true blue	white	67–70	slip	mauve	
9–12	slip	mermaid		71–72	Fair Isle	mauve	white
13–14	Fair Isle	mermaid	white	73–76	slip	strawberry	
15–18	slip	mauve		77–78	Fair Isle	strawberry	white
19–20	Fair Isle	mauve	white	79–82	slip	spode blue	
21–24	slip	spode blue		83–84	Fair Isle	spode blue	white
25–26	Fair Isle	spode blue	white	85–88	slip	polka	
27–30	slip	strawberry		89–92	Fair Isle	strawberry	white
31–32	Fair Isle	strawberry	white	93–96	slip	lilac	
33–36	slip	mermaid		97	Fair Isle	lilac	white
37–40	Fair Isle	polka	white	98	Fair Isle	spode blue	white
41–44	slip	strawberry		99–102	slip	spode blue	
45	Fair Isle	strawberry	white	103–104	Fair Isle	polka	white
46	Fair Isle	spode blue	white	105–108	slip	blue scan	
47–50	slip	spode blue		Repeat rows 5 to 108 throughout.			

SWEATER BACK
Bring forward 142 (150, 158) needles on each bed to WP. Arrange needles for 1 × 1 rib.
Using white cast on, ending with carriage at right.
MT–3, knit 40 rows.
Work 6 rows waste yarn and release work from machine.
Bring forward 160 (168, 176) needles on main bed to WP.
Hook sts from last row worked in white evenly over the needles, increasing sts as necessary along the bed. Insert punchcard and lock on first row of pattern.
Set patt into memory. RC 000. MT.
Working patt sequence as given in chart, knit to RC 158 (162, 166).
Shape armholes
Keeping patt sequence correct, cast off (bind off) 5 sts at beg of next 2 rows. 150 (158, 166) sts.
Knit to RC 324 (332, 340).
Shape shoulders
Cast off (bind off) 14 (15, 16) sts at beg of next 4 rows, then 15 (16, 17) sts at beg of foll 2 rows.
Cast off (bind off) rem 64 (66, 68) sts.

SWEATER FRONT
Work as given for back until RC 296 (304, 312).
Carriage at right.
Shape neck
Note row on punchcard.
With a spare length of white cast off (bind off) centre 10 (12, 14) sts.
Push all needles at left of needlebed to HP.
Work on first side of neck as follows:
Patt 1 row.
Keeping patt sequence correct, cast off (bind off) 3 sts at beg of next and foll 2 alt rows, then 2 sts at beg of foll 9 alt rows. 43 (46, 49) sts. RC 320 (328, 336).
Knit to RC 326 (334, 342).
Shape shoulder
Cast off (bind off) 14 (15, 16) sts at beg of next and foll alt row.
Knit 1 row, then cast off (bind off).
Return punchcard to row number previously noted.
Set patt into memory.
Return needles at left to WP.
Complete to match first side of neck, reversing all shaping.

1

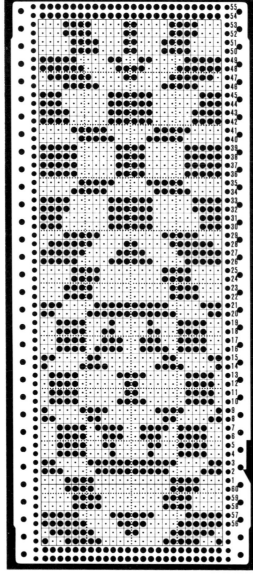

2

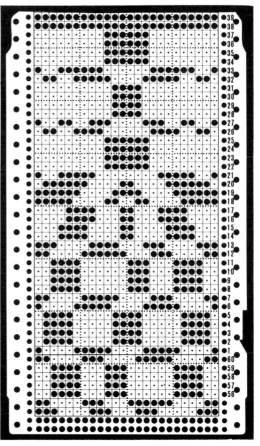

61(63, 64)cm/
24 (25, 25¼)in

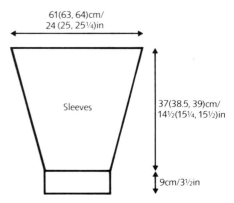

Sleeves

37(38.5, 39)cm/
14½(15¼, 15½)in

9cm/3½in

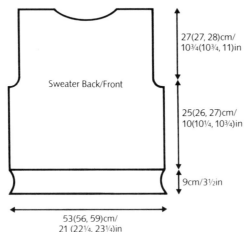

27(27, 28)cm/
10¾(10¾, 11)in

Sweater Back/Front

25(26, 27)cm/
10(10¼, 10¾)in

9cm/3½in

53(56, 59)cm/
21 (22¼, 23¼)in

SWEATER SLEEVES
Bring forward 74 (76, 78) needles on each bed to WP.
Arrange needles for 1 × 1 rib.
Using white cast on, ending with carriage at right.
MT–3, knit 40 rows.
Work 6 rows waste yarn and release work from
machine.
Bring forward 94 (96, 98) needles on main bed to WP.
Carriage at right.
With WS of work facing, hook sts from last row worked
in white evenly over the needles, increasing sts as
necessary along the bed.
Insert punchcard and lock on first row of pattern.
Set patt into memory. RC 000. MT.
Working patt sequence as given in chart for sleeves, inc
1 st each end of every 5th row until there are 184 (188,
192) sts. RC 225 (230, 235).
Knit straight to RC 232 (240, 248).
Cast off (bind off) loosely.

SWEATER NECKBAND
Bring forward 126 (130, 134) needles on each bed to
WP. Arrange needles for 2 × 2 rib.
Using white cast on, ending with carriage at right.
MT–3, knit 10 rows.
Work 6 rows waste yarn and release work from
machine.

TO MAKE UP
Join shoulder seams. Folds sleeves in half lengthwise,
then placing folds to shoulder seams, sew into position.
Join side and sleeve seams. Join neckband seam. Pin
neckband into position, then, carefully removing waste
yarn as necessary, sew neckband to neck edge by
backstitching through the open sts one by one.

CARDIGAN

Work back and sleeves as given for sweater.

CARDIGAN RIGHT FRONT

Bring forward 71 (75, 78) needles on each bed to WP.
Arrange needles for 1 × 1 rib.
Using white cast on, ending with carriage at right.
MT−3, knit 40 rows.
Work 6 rows waste yarn and release work from machine.
Bring forward 80 (84, 88) needles on main bed to WP.
Hook sts from last row worked in white evenly over the needles, increasing sts as necessary along the bed. Insert punchcard and lock on first row of pattern.
Set patt into memory. RC 000. MT.
Working patt sequence as given in chart, knit to RC 158 (162, 166).
Shape armhole
Keeping patt sequence correct, cast off (bind off) 5 sts at beg of next row. 75 (79, 83) sts.
Shape front neck
Dec 1 st at left on next and every foll 5th row until 43 (46, 49) sts rem.
Knit to RC 324 (332, 340).
Shape shoulder
Cast off (bind off) 14 (15, 16) sts at beg of next and foll alt row.
Patt 1 row, then cast off (bind off) rem sts.

CARDIGAN LEFT FRONT

Work as given for right front, reversing all shaping.

BUTTON AND BUTTONHOLE BORDER

Bring foward 14 needles on each bed to WP.

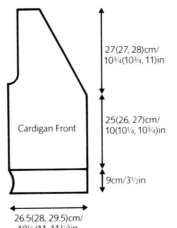

27(27, 28)cm/
10¾(10¾, 11)in

Cardigan Front

25(26, 27)cm/
10(10¼, 10¾)in

9cm/3½in

26.5(28, 29.5)cm/
10½(11, 11¾)in

Using white cast on, ending with carriage at right.
RC 000. MT−3. Knit to RC 4.
* Using a spare length of white, cast off (bind off) centre 4 sts, then using the same length of yarn, cast them on again over the same 4 needles, knit 28 rows.
Rep from * 4 times more, then knit to RC 460.
Cast off (bind off) using the latchet hook.

TO MAKE UP

Join shoulder seams. Folds sleeves in half lengthwise, then placing folds to shoulder seams, sew into position.
Join side and sleeve seams.
Sew on button and buttonhole border, stretching slightly as necessary. Sew on buttons.

Above: Knitted in different colours, the cardigan version of Jamie and Jessi Seaton's Paperchains is shown here.

JAMIE AND JESSI SEATON

CHEVRONS

MATERIALS
Rowan Botany 4 ply
250 (275, 275)g/9½ (10, 10)oz in black (shade 62)
25g/1oz in sea green (shade 91)
125 (125, 150)g/5 (5, 6)oz in dark grey (shade 635)
25 (25, 50)g/1 (1, 2)oz in airforce blue (shade 108)
25g/1oz in bright blue (shade 55)
25g/1oz in magenta (shade 631)
25g/1oz in red (shade 45)
25g/1oz in scarlet (shade 44)
25g/1oz in ginger (shade 26)
25g/1oz in lilac (shade 121)
25 (50, 50)g/1 (2,2)oz in dark blue (shade 54)
25g/1oz in royal (shade 56)
Rowan Fine Fleck Tweed
25g/1oz in emerald (shade 124)
25g/1oz in silver (shade 64)

MEASUREMENTS
To fit bust/chest 91 (97, 102)cm/36 (38, 40) in
Actual size
Bust/chest 102 (106, 112) cm/40 (42, 44) in
Length 66 cm/26 in
Sleeve seam 46 cm/18 in

TENSION
32 sts and 40 rows to 10cm/4in worked over Fair Isle
with TD at approx 8

MACHINE
Any Brother standard gauge electronic or punchcard
machine with ribbing attachment or equivalent. (If
ribbing attachment not available see alternative methods
of ribbing techniques – p.123).

PATCHES
No 1 (make 4)
Bring forward 17 needles on main bed to WP.
Cast on with waste yarn and knit 6 rows.
Insert punchcard 6 and lock on first row of patt.
Using silver, knit 4 rows. MT.
Set machine for Fair Isle.
With silver in feeder A, knit 7 rows bright blue in feeder
B, then 4 rows airforce blue, 4 rows royal and 5 rows
bright blue.
Set machine for plain knitting.
Knit 3 rows silver.
Using waste yarn, knit 6 rows.
Release sts from machine.

No 2 (make 7)
Work as given for patch 1, using airforce blue in feeder A
and 7 rows bright blue, 4 rows lilac, 4 rows sliver and 5
rows bright blue in feeder B.

No 3 (make 4)
Work as given for patch 1, using dark blue in feeder A
and 7 rows royal, 4 rows airforce blue, 4 rows bright blue
and 5 rows royal in feeder B.

BACK
Bring forward 164 (170, 178) needles on each bed to
WP. Arrange needles for 1 × 1 rib.
Using black cast on, ending with carriage at right.
MT–3, knit 14 rows. Transfer all sts to main bed.
Insert punchcards 1, 2, 3, 4 and 5 (joined together) and
lock on first row of pattern.
Set patt into memory. RC 000.
MT. Working patt sequence as given in chart, knit to RC
146.

*Left: The little tulip motif
patches are knitted first and
left on waste yarn, then
worked into the jersey
when the main fabric is
being knitted.*

PATTERN SEQUENCE FOR BACK, FRONT AND SLEEVES

ROWS	PATTERN SETTING	COLOUR IN FEEDER A	COLOUR IN FEEDER B
Join together punchcards 1, 2, 3, 4 and 5 in sequence			
1–6	plain	black	
Release card			
7–12	Fair Isle	black	emerald
13–18	''	black	sea green
19–20	''	dark grey	sea green
21–24	''	dark grey	emerald
25–28	''	black	emerald
29–33	''	black	sea green
34–36	''	dark grey	sea green
37–38	''	dark grey	silver
39–41	''	black	silver
42–44	''	black	airforce blue
45–48	''	black	bright blue
49	''	black	magenta
50–52	''	black	bright blue
53–56	''	black	airforce blue
57–59	''	dark grey	airforce blue
60	plain	dark grey	
61–63	Fair Isle	dark grey	red
64	''	dark grey	magenta
65	''	dark grey	scarlet
66–68	''	dark grey	ginger
69–70	plain	dark grey	
71	''	lilac	
72	''	silver	
73	''	bright blue	
74	''	dark blue	
75	Fair Isle	dark blue	magenta
76–78	''	dark blue	red
79	plain	dark blue	
80	''	royal	
81	''	black	
82–87	Fair Isle	black	dark grey

Place patches for back and front (see pattern)
Patch No 2 over needles 55–39 at left, patch No 1 over needles 8 at left to 9 at right and patch No 2 over needles 40–56 at right.
Place patches for sleeves
Patch No 2 over needles 43–27 at left and patch No 1 over needles 27–43 at right.

ROWS	PATTERN SETTING	COLOUR IN FEEDER A	COLOUR IN FEEDER B
88–119	Fair Isle	black	dark grey
Pick up patches (see pattern)			
120–125	''	black	dark grey
126	plain	black	
127	''	ginger	
128	''	airforce blue	

ROWS	PATTERN SETTING	COLOUR IN FEEDER A	COLOUR IN FEEDER B
129	''	royal	
130	''	dark blue	
131	Fair Isle	dark blue	magenta
132–133	''	dark blue	red
134	''	dark blue	scarlet
135	plain	dark blue	
136	''	bright blue	
137–138	''	black	
139–147	Fair Isle	black	emerald
148–149	''	black	sea green
150–153	''	dark grey	sea green
154–155	''	dark grey	emerald
156–158	''	black	emerald
159–163	''	black	silver
164–167	''	black	bright blue
168–171	''	black	airforce blue
172–173	''	black	bright blue
174–176	''	dark grey	bright blue
177–178	plain	dark grey	
179	''	lilac	
180	''	magenta	
181	''	silver	
182	''	dark blue	
183–187	Fair Isle	dark blue	black
188		red	black
189–190	''	airforce blue	black
191	''	magenta	black
192–195	''	dark grey	black
196	plain	dark grey	
197–202	Fair Isle	dark grey	black

Place patches on back and front (see pattern)
Patch No 3 over needles 55–39 at left, patch No 2 (back only) over needles 8 at left to 9 at right, patch No 3 over needles 40–56 at right.

ROWS	PATTERN SETTING	COLOUR IN FEEDER A	COLOUR IN FEEDER B
203–234	Fair Isle	dark grey	black
Pick up patches (see pattern)			
235–240	Fair Isle	dark grey	black
241	plain	dark grey	
242	''	red	
243	''	royal	
244	''	airforce blue	
245	''	dark blue	
246	Fair Isle	dark blue	ginger
247	''	dark blue	magenta
248–249	''	dark blue	scarlet
250	plain	dark blue	
251	''	lilac	
252–256	''	black	

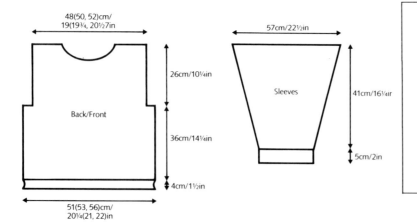

48(50, 52)cm/
19(19¾, 20½7in

26cm/10¼in

Back/Front

36cm/14¼in

4cm/1½in

51(53, 56)cm/
20¼(21, 22)in

57cm/22½in

Sleeves

41cm/16¼in

5cm/2in

To place patches
Using waste yarn knit the sts, over the needles given, by hand, taking the needles back to NWP. Lift off the long loops formed. With RS of patch facing and with motif upside down, pick up the first row of sts in main yarn and place on to empty needles. Remove waste yarn. Replace removed sts back on to needles and continue knitting.

To pick up patches
Remove same sts as before on to waste yarn. With WS of same patch facing, pick up last row of sts in main yarn and place on to needles. Replace removed sts back on to needles and continue knitting.

Left: Bands of chevrons are separated by colourful borders of hearts and flowers on these unusual sweaters designed by Jamie and Jessi Seaton.

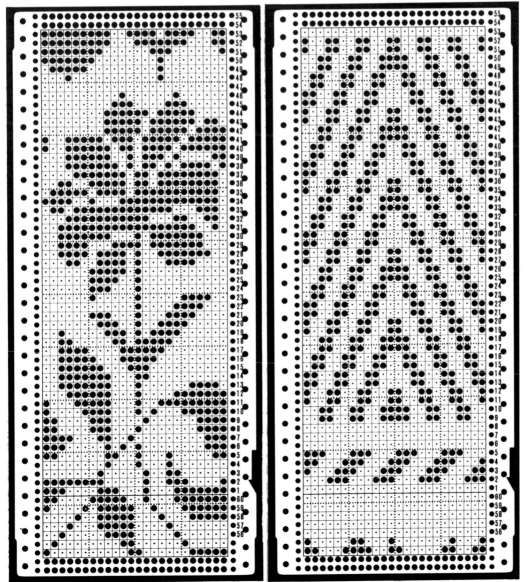

Jamie and Jessi Seaton

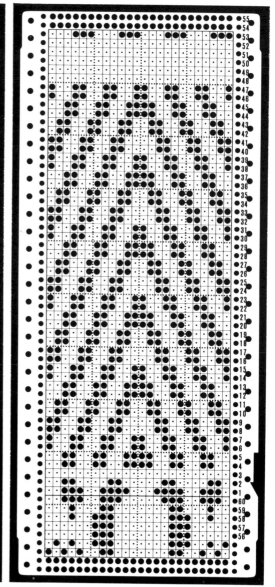

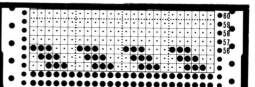

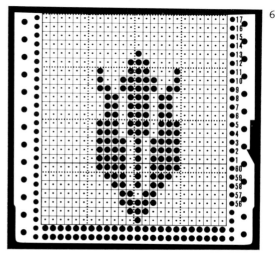

Shape armholes
Keeping patt sequence correct, cast off 5 sts at beg of
next 2 rows. 154 (160, 168) sts.
Knit to RC 250.
Cast off 15 (16, 18) sts at beg of next 4 rows, then 16
(17, 17) sts at beg of foll 2 rows. RC 256.
Cast off rem 62 sts.

FRONT
Work as given for back until RC 224.
Carriage at right.
Shape neck
Note row on punchcard.
With a spare length of yarn, cast off centre 18 sts.
Push all needles at left of needlebed to HP.
Work on first side of neck as follows;
Patt 1 row.
Cast off 3 sts at beg of next and foll 5 alt rows.
RC 236.
Then cast off 2 sts at beg of foll 2 alt rows.
RC 240. 46 (49, 53) sts.
Return punchcard to row number previously noted.
Set patt into memory. RC 224.
Return needles at left to WP.
Complete to match first side of neck, reversing all
shaping.

SLEEVES
Bring forward 70 needles on each bed to WP. Arrange

Left: Knitting in paler colours creates a different, but just as attractive garment.

needles for 1 × 1 rib.
Using black cast on, ending with carriage at right.
MT−3, knit 20 rows.
Work 6 rows waste yarn and release work from machine.
Bring forward 84 needles on main bed to WP.
Carriage at right.
With WS of work facing, hook sts from last row worked in black evenly over the needles, increasing sts as necessary along the bed.
Insert punchcards 1, 2, 3, 4 and 5 (joined together) and lock on first row of pattern.
MT. RC 000. Increasing 1 st each end of every 3rd row, knit 16 rows black.
Set patt into memory.
Working patt sequence as given in chart, cont to inc 1 st each end of every 3rd row until there are 184 sts.
Knit straight to RC 152.
Continuing in black only, knit to RC 164.
Cast off loosely.

NECKBAND
Bring forward 150 needles on each bed to WP.
Arrange needles for 1 × 1 rib.
Using black cast on, ending with carriage at right.
MT−3, knit 11 rows. Carriage at left.
Transfer all sts to main bed.
With WS of back facing, pick up 50 sts across back neck and place on to first 50 needles of neckband, placing sts over top of neckband sts. With WS of front facing, pick up 35 sts down first side of neck, 20 sts from centre front and 35 sts up second side of neck and hook on to needles. 150 sts.
MT + 1. Knit 1 row.
Cast off loosely.

COLLAR
Bring forward 156 needles on each bed to WP.
Arrange needles for 1 × 1 rib.
Using black cast on, ending with carriage at right.
MT−3, knit 48 rows.
Transfer all sts to main bed.
Cast off loosely.

TO MAKE UP
Join shoulder and neckband seams. Sew collar to inner edge of neckband, beginning and ending at centre front. Fold sleeves in half lengthwise, then placing folds to shoulder seams, sew into position. Join side and sleeve seams.

CHRISTOPHER FISCHER

MUSHROOM AND PINK COTTON

Right: The little fisherman's rib collar adds a special touch to this cotton sweater.

MATERIALS
Rowan Sea Breeze
125 (150) g/5 (6) oz in ecru (shade 522)
125 (150) g/5 (6) oz in pink (shade 533)
Rowan Cabled Mercerised Cotton
50g/2oz in lichen (shade 327)
125 (150) g/5 (6) oz in mushroom (shade 325)
225 (250) g/9 (9½) ox in pale pink (shade 328)
Rowan Cotton Glacé
225 (250) g/9 (9½) oz in sweat pea (shade 728)

MEASUREMENTS
To fit bust 81–91 (97–102)cm/34–36 (38–40) in
Actual size

Bust 106 (114) cm/42 (45) in
Length 59cm/23½in
Sleeve seam 38.5cm/15¼in

TENSION
31 sts and 37 rows to 10cm/4in worked over st st with TD at approx 8

MACHINE
Any Brother standard gauge electronic or punchcard machine with ribbing attachment or equivalent
(If ribbing attachment not available see Alternative methods of ribbing in techniques – p.123)

PATTERN SEQUENCE FOR BACK AND FRONT

ROWS	PATTERN SETTING	COLOUR IN FEEDER A	COLOUR IN FEEDER B	ROWS	PATTERN SETTING	COLOUR IN FEEDER A	COLOUR IN FEEDER B
1	Fair Isle	pink	lichen	113	''	pink	lichen
2–8	''	pink	pale pink	114–120	''	pink	pale pink
9	''	mushroom	lichen	121	''	mushroom	lichen
10–16	''	mushroom	sweet pea	122–144	''	mushroom	sweet pea
17	''	ecru	lichen	145	''	ecru	lichen
18–24	''	ecru	pink	146–152	''	ecru	pink
25	''	pale pink	lichen	153	''	pale pink	lichen
26–48	''	pale pink	mushroom	154–160	''	pale pink	mushroom
49	''	sweet pea	lichen	161	''	sweet pea	lichen
50–56	''	sweet pea	ecru	162–168	''	sweet pea	ecru
57	''	pink	lichen	169	''	pink	lichen
58–64	''	pink	pale pink	170–192	''	pink	pale pink
65	''	mushroom	lichen	193	''	mushroom	lichen
66–72	''	mushroom	sweet pea	194–200	''	mushroom	sweet pea
73	''	ecru	lichen	201	''	ecru	lichen
74–96	''	ecru	pink	202–208	''	ecru	pink
97	''	pale pink	lichen	209	''	pale pink	lichen
98–104	''	pale pink	mushroom	210–216	''	pale pink	mushroom
105	''	sweet pea	lichen	217	''	sweet pea	lichen
106–112	''	sweet pea	ecru	218	''	sweet pea	ecru

BACK
Bring forward 154 (166) needles on each bed to WP.
Arrange needles for 1 + 1 rib.
Using pale pink cast on, ending with carriage at right.
MT–4, knit 14 rows.
Work 6 rows waste yarn and release work from machine.
Bring forward 164 (176) needles on main bed to WP.
Carriage at right.
With WS of work facing, hook sts from last row worked in pale pink evenly over the needles, increasing sts as necessary along the bed.
Insert punchcard (joined into a circle) and lock on first row of pattern.
Set patt into memory. RC 000.
Set machine for Fair Isle. MT.
Working patt sequence as given in chart, inc 1 st each end of every 7th row until there are 184 (196) sts.
RC 70.
Knit to RC 98.
Shape armholes.
Keeping patt sequence correct and using triple transfer tool, dec 2 sts each end of next and every foll 3rd row until 160 (172) sts rem. RC 114. Knit to RC 210.
Shape shoulders
Push 8 needles at opposite end to carriage into HP on next 6 rows, then 9 needles on foll 4 rows.
Cast off (bind off) rem 76 (88) sts.
Return 42 needles at left into WP. Using waste yarn, knit 6 rows.
Release sts from machine.
Return rem sts to WP. Using waste yarn, knit 6 rows.
Release sts from machine.

FRONT
Work as given for back until RC 192.
Carriage at right.
Shape neck
Note row on punchcard.
Cast off (bind off) centre 44 (52) needles into HP.
Push all needles at left of needlebed to HP.
Work on first ide of neck as follows:
Using triple transfer tool, dec 2 sts at neck edge on every alt row until 42 sts rem. RC 208 (210).
Knit straight to RC 218.
Using waste yarn, knit 6 rows.
Release sts from machine.
Return punchcard to row number previously noted.
Set patt into memory. RC 192.
Return needles at left to WP.
Complete to match first side of neck, reversing all shaping.

PATTERN SEQUENCE FOR SLEEVES

ROWS	PATTERN SETTING	COLOUR IN FEEDER A	COLOUR IN FEEDER B	ROWS	PATTERN SETTING	COLOUR IN FEEDER A	COLOUR IN FEEDER B
1-4	Fair Isle	ecru	pink	85	,,	sweet pea	lichen
5	,,	pale pink	lichen	86–92	,,	sweet pea	ecru
6–12	,,	pale pink	mushroom	93	,,	pink	lichen
13	,,	sweet pea	lichen	94–100	,,	pink	pale pink
14–36	,,	sweet pea	ecru	101	,,	mushroom	lichen
37	,,	pink	lichen	102–108	,,	mushroom	sweet pea
38–44	,,	pink	pale pink	109	,,	ecru	lichen
45	,,	mushroom	lichen	110–132	,,	ecru	pink
46–52	,,	mushroom	sweet pea	133	,,	pale pink	lichen
53	,,	ecru	lichen	134–140	,,	pale pink	mushroom
54–60	,,	ecru	pink	141	,,	sweet pea	lichen
61	,,	pale pink	lichen	142–148	,,	sweet pea	ecru
62–84	,,	pale pink	mushroom	149	,,	pink	lichen
				150–154	,,	pink	pale pink

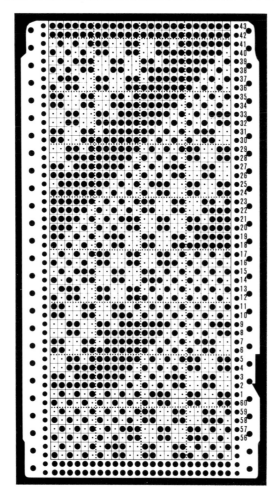

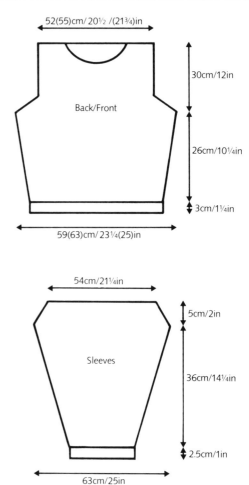

52(55)cm/20½ /(21¾)in

30cm/12in

Back/Front

26cm/10¼in

3cm/1¼in

59(63)cm/23¼(25)in

54cm/21¼in

5cm/2in

Sleeves

36cm/14¼in

2.5cm/1in

63cm/25in

SLEEVES

Bring forward 90 needles on each bed to WP. Arrange needles for 1 × 1 rib.
Using pale pink cast on, ending with carriage at right.
MT-4, knit 10 rows.
Transfer all sts to main bed.
Insert punchcard and lock on first row of pattern.
Set patt into memory. RC 000.
Set machine for Fair Isle. MT.
Working patt sequence as given in chart for sleeves, inc 1 st each end of every alt row until there are 152 sts, then each end of evey foll 3rd row until there are 196 sts. Knit straight to RC 134.
Shape top.
Using triple transfer tool, dec 2 sts each end of next and every foll 3rd row until 168 sts rem.
Knit 1 row. RC 154.
Cast off (bind off) loosely.

COLLAR

Bring forward 160 needles on each bed to WP.
Arrange needles for 1 × 1 rib.
Using pale pink cast on, and end with the carriage at the right.
Set machine to alternately knit 1 row and tuck 1 row on main bed, and knit every row on rib bed to form fisherman's rib.
MT–3, knit 38 rows fisherman's rib.
Now work 6 rows plain rib.
Cast off (bind off) loosely.

Left: The beautiful pastel shades of cotton subtly blend together on this classic jersey by Christopher Fischer.

TO MAKE UP
With RS of back facing, replace sts of both shoulders on to needles and remove waste yarn. Push sts back behind latches.
With WS of front facing, place sts of both shoulders on to same needles holding sts of back shoulders, leaving the sts in the hooks, then remove waste yarn.
Carefully push back each needle, so pulling sts of front shoulders through sts of back shoulders.
Using pale pink, cast off (bind off) each set of shoulder sts.
Folds sleeves in half lengthwise, then placing folds to shoulder seams, sew into position. Join side and sleeve seams.
Sew cast-off edge of collar in place, joining for 1cm/½in at centre front.

CHRISTOPHER FISCHER

TARTAN SWEATER

Right: Work as given in pattern, shown here in the man's sweater, or knit in softer tones and work a crew neck by knitting fewer rows on the collar.

MATERIALS
Rowan Botany 4 ply
25g/1oz in magenta (shade 96)
25g/1oz in mustard (shade 9)
25g/1oz in airforce blue (shade 108)
25g/1oz in royal blue (shade 56)
25g/1oz in green (shade 100)
75 (100, 100) g/3 (4, 4) oz in white (shade 1)
Rowan Light Tweed
25g/1oz in rosemix (shade 215)
100 (125, 125) g/4 (5, 5) oz in silver (shade 208)
150 (175, 175) g/6 (7, 7) oz in black (shade 211)
100 (100, 125) g/4 (4, 5) oz in ebony (shade 207)
75 (100, 100) g/3 (4, 4) oz in grey (shade 209)

MEASUREMENTS
To fit chest 102 (112, 122) cm/40 (44, 48) in
Actual size
Chest 110 (120, 126) cm/43½ (47½, 50) in
Length 67cm/26½in
Sleeve seam 47cm/18½in

TENSION
30 sts and 36 rows to 10cm/4in worked over Fair Isle with TD at approx 9

MACHINE
Any Brother standard gauge electronic or punchcard machine with ribbing attachment or equivalent (If ribbing attachment not available – see Alternative methods of ribbing in techniques – p.123)

PATTERN SEQUENCE FOR BACK AND FRONT

ROWS	PATTERN SETTING	COLOUR IN FEEDER A	COLOUR IN FEEDER B	ROWS	PATTERN SETTING	COLOUR IN FEEDER A	COLOUR IN FEEDER B
Join card into a circle				73	''	black	green
Release card				74–96	''	black	silver
				97	''	white	mustard
1	Fair Isle	silver	rosemix	98-104	''	white	ebony
2–8	''	silver	white	105	''	grey	airforce blue
9	''	ebony	magenta	106–112	''	grey	black
10–16	''	ebony	grey	113	''	silver	rosemix
17	''	black	green	114–120	''	silver	white
18–24	''	black	silver	121	''	ebony	magenta
25	''	white	mustard	122–144	''	ebony	grey
26–48	''	white	ebony	145	''	black	green
49	''	grey	airforce blue	146–152	''	black	silver
50–56	''	grey	black	153	''	white	mustard
57	''	silver	rosemix	154–160	''	white	ebony
58–64	''	silver	white	161	''	grey	airforce blue
65	''	ebony	magenta	162–168	''	grey	black
66–72	''	ebony	grey	169	''	silver	rosemix
				170–192	''	silver	white

BACK
* Bring forward 137 (153, 152) needles on each bed to WP. Arrange needles for 1 × 1 rib.
Using airforce blue cast on, ending with carriage at right. RC 000. MT–3, knit 3 rows.
Change to black and knit 14 rows. RC 17.
Change to rosemix and knit 4 rows. RC 21.
Change to black and knit 21 rows. RC 42.
Work 6 rows waste yarn and release work from machine.
Bring forward 148 (164, 172) needles on main bed to WP. Carriage at right.
With WS of work facing, hook sts from last row worked in black evenly over the needles, increasing sts as necessary along the bed. *
Counting from the centre 0 transfer the sts from the 18th, 42nd and 66th needles at left of centre and the 20th, 44th and 68th needles at right of centre on to their adjacent needles. Push the empty needles back into NWP.
Insert punchcard with A side facing and lock on first row of pattern.
Set patt into memory. RC 000.
MT. Working patt sequence as given in chart and increasing 1 st each end on rows 3, 6, 10, 14, 19, 24, 30 and 36, knit to RC 110.

Shape armholes
Keeping patt sequence correct and bringing into WP the needles pushed back into NWP as necessary, cast off (bind off) 2 sts at beg of next 2 rows.
Knit 2 rows. RC 114.
Using triple transfer tool, dec 1 st each end of next and every foll alt row until 154 (170, 178) sts rem. RC 119.
Knit 1 row. RC 120.
Using triple transfer tool, dec 1 st each end of next and every foll 3rd row until 104 (120, 128) sts rem.
Knit to RC 192.
Using separate lengths of black yarn, cast off (bind off) 33 (41, 45) sts at left and 33 (41, 45) sts at right for shoulders.
Using waste yarn, knit 6 rows over rem needles.
Release sts from machine.

FRONT
Work as given for back from * to *.
Counting from the centre 0 transfer the sts from the 20th, 44th and 68th needles at left of centre and the 18th, 42nd and 66th needles at right of centre on to their adjacent needles. Push the empty needles back into NWP.
Insert punchcard with opposite side to A facing and lock on first row of pattern.

PATTERN SEQUENCE FOR SLEEVES

ROWS	PATTERN SETTING	COLOUR IN FEEDER A	COLOUR IN FEEDER B	ROWS	PATTERN SETTING	COLOUR IN FEEDER A	COLOUR IN FEEDER B
Join card into a circle				119	,,	grey	airforce blue
Release card				120–126	,,	grey	black
				127	,,	silver	rosemix
1-14	Fair Isle	grey	black	128–134	,,	silver	white
15	,,	silver	rosemix	135	,,	ebony	magenta
16–22	,,	silver	white	136–158	,,	ebony	grey
23	,,	ebony	magenta	159	,,	black	green
24–30	,,	ebony	grey	160–166	,,	black	silver
31	,,	black	green	167		white	mustard
32–38	,,	black	silver	168–174	,,	white	ebony
39	,,	white	mustard	175	,,	grey	airforce blue
40–62	,,	white	ebony	176–182	,,	grey	black
63	,,	grey	airforce blue	183	,,	silver	rosemix
64–70	,,	grey	black	184–206	,,	silver	white
71	,,	silver	rosemix	207	,,	ebony	magenta
72–78	,,	silver	white	208–214	,,	ebony	grey
79	,,	ebony	magenta	215	,,	black	green
80–86	,,	ebony	grey	216–222	,,	black	silver
87	,,	black	green	223	,,	white	mustard
88–110	,,	black	silver	224–230	,,	white	ebony
111	,,	white	mustard	231	,,	grey	airforce blue
112–118	,,	white	ebony	232–254	,,	grey	black

Set patt into memory. RC 000.
MT. Now cont as given for back to RC 186.
104 (120, 128) sts. Carriage at right.
Note row on punchcard.
Shape neck
Place centre 26 needles into HP.
Push all needles at left of needlebed to HP.
Work on first side of neck as follows:
Decreasing 1 st at both edges on RC 186, 188 and 190,
knot to RC 192.
Cast off (bind off).
Return 26 centre sts to WP.
Using waste yarn, knit 6 rows. Release sts from machine.
Return punchcard to row number previously noted.
Set patt into memory.
Return needles at left to WP.
Complete to match first side of neck, reversing all
shaping.

SLEEVES
Bring forward 74 needles on each bed to WP. Arrange
needles for 1 × 1 rib.
Cast on and work 42 rows as given for back.
Work 6 rows waste yarn and release work from
machine.
Bring forward 84 needles on main bed to WP.
Carriage at right.
With WS of work facing, hook sts from last row worked
in black evenly over the needles, increasing sts as
necessary along the bed.
Insert punchcard with A side facing and lock on row 35
of pattern.
Counting from the centre 0 transfer the sts from the
18th needle at left of centre and the 20th needle at right
of centre on to their adjacent needles. Push the empty
needles back into NWP.
Set patt into memory. RC 000.
MT. Working patt sequence as given in chart for sleeves,
inc 1 st each end of every alt row until there are 118 sts.
RC 34.
Now inc 1 st each end of every foll 3rd row until there
are 174 sts. RC 119.
Knit straight to RC 124.
Shape top
Keeping patt sequence correct and bringing into WP the
needles pushed back into NWP as necessary, cast off
(bind off) 2 sts at beg of next 2 rows.
Knit 2 rows. RC 128.
Using triple transfer tool, dec 1 st each end of every row

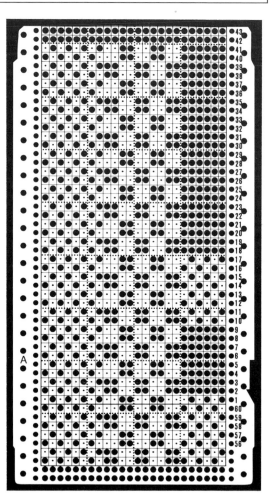

until 58 sts rem. RC 183.
Knit 1 row. RC 184.
Using triple transfer tool, dec 1 st each end of next and
every foll alt row until 26 sts rem.
Knit straight o RC 254.
Using waste yarn, knit 6 rows. Release sts from machine.
Work second sleeve the same as first, reversing
punchcard before beg of patt.

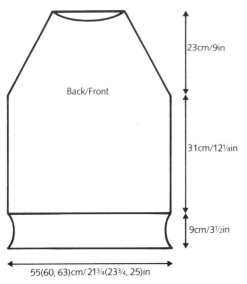

Back/Front

23cm/9in

31cm/12¼in

9cm/3½in

55(60, 63)cm/21¾(23¾, 25)in

8cm/3¼in

Sleeves

13cm/5¼in

23cm/9¼in

36cm/14¼in

9cm/3½in

58cm/23in

Above: You may find it easier to use a crochet hook to work the coloured chains forming the design on the Tartan Sweater, shown here with Jane Davies' Scarp sweater.

COLLAR
Bring forward 132 needles on each bed to WP.
Arrange needles for 1 × 1 rib.
Using black cast on, ending with carriage at right.
Set machine for fisherman's rib, with all needles knitting of ribber bed and tucking every alt row on main bed.
MT−3, knit 7 rows.
Change to blue and knit 6 rows.
Change to black and knit to RC 81.
Carriage at left.
Transfer all sts to main bed.
With WS of back facing, hook 38 sts held on waste yarn at back neck on to first 38 needles of neckband, placing sts over top of neckband sts, then with WS of first sleeve facing hook 26 sts held on waste yarn at top of sleeve extension on to next 26 needles. With WS of front facing, pick up 8 sts down first side of neck and place on to next 8 needles of neckband, hook 26 sts from waste yarn at centre front on to needles, then pick up 8 sts up second side of neck and hook on to needles. Hook 26 sts of 2nd sleeve on to remaining 26 needles. 132 sts.

MT + 1. Knit 1 row black.
Cast off (bind off) loosely.

TO MAKE UP
Sew row ends of sleeve extensions to cast-off sts of shoulders on back and front. Join raglan armhole seams, then join side and sleeve seams. Join collar seam.
Using magenta and chain st, embroider a line down first ladder at left of front. Miss next ladder, then work first a royal blue line, then a magenta line down next 2 ladders. Miss next ladder then work a royal blue line over last ladder. Repeat embroidery on same ladders at back and over one ladder on each of the sleeves.
Using 2 strands of ebony, 2 strands of black, 1 strand of silver and 1 strand of mustard together, embroider remaining ladders by working a whipping st over the sts each side of the ladder to form a chunky 'cable'.

PASTEL SHELLS SWEATER

Right: Ten different colours are used to produce the softly coloured shell motifs against a white background on this lovely cotton sweater.

MATERIALS
Rowan Sea Breeze
255 (280, 315) g/9 (10, 11) oz in bleached white (Shade 521)
20 (25, 30) g/¾ (1, 1½) oz in smoke (shade 527)
20 (25, 25) g/¾ (1, 1) oz in pine (shade 538)
Rowan Cabled Mercerised Cotton
50 (55, 60) g/2 (2, 2½) oz in pale mauve (shade 311)
50g/2oz in silver lining (shade 316)
50g/2oz in pastel peach (shade 313)
50g/2oz in pale pink (shade 328)
Rowan Salad Days
50g/2oz in linen (shade 562)
Rowan Fine Cotton Chenille
20 (25, 25) g/¾ (1, 1) oz in turquoise (shade 383)
10 (12, 15) g/½ (½, ¾) oz in aqua (shade 390)
20 (25, 25) g/¾ (1, 1) oz in carnation (shade 389)

MEASUREMENTS
To fit bust 81–86 (91–97, 102–107) cm/32–34 (36–38, 40–42) in
Actual size
Bust 94 (104, 114) cm/37 (41, 45) in
Length 65cm/25½in
Sleeve seam 48cm/19in

TENSION
31 sts and 39 rows to 10cm/4in worked over Fair Isle with TD and approx 7

MACHINE
Any Brother standard gauge electronic or punchcard machine with ribbing attachment or equvalent
(If ribbing attachment not available see Alternative methods of ribbing in techniques – p.123)

PATTERN SEQUENCE FOR BACK, FRONT AND SLEEVES

ROWS	PATTERN SETTING	COLOUR IN FEEDER A	COLOUR IN FEEDER B	ROWS	PATTERN SETTING	COLOUR IN FEEDER A	COLOUR IN FEEDER B
Punchcard 1 – border patt				Punchcard 2 (joined into a circle)			
1	plain	smoke		15–20	plain	white	
Release card				21–22	Fair Isle	white	turquoise
2–3	Fair Isle	white	pastel peach	23–25	,,	,,	pine
4	plain	smoke		26	,,	,,	aqua
5–6	Fair Isle	white	pale mauve	27–28	,,	,,	smoke
7–8	,,	,,	silver lining	29–32	,,	,,	pale mauve
9–10	,,	,,	linen	33–34	,,	,,	silver lining
11	plain	smoke		35–36	,,	,,	linen
12–13	Fair Isle	white	pastel peach	37–38	,,	,,	carnation
14	plain	white		39–40	,,	,,	pastel peach
				41–45	,,	,,	pale pink
				46–50	plain	white	
				Rep rows 21 to 50 to the end.			

BACK
Bring forward 145 (161, 178) needles on each bed to WP. Arrange needles for 1 × 1 rib.
Using white cast on, ending with carriage at right.
RC 000
MT−4, knit 26 rows. RC 26
Transfer all sts to main bed. 145 (161, 178) sts.
Insert punchcard 1 and lock on first row of pattern.
Set patt into memory. RC 000.
Working patt sequence as given in chart, knit to RC 132
Shape armholes
Keeping pattern sequence correct, cast off (bind off) 12 sts at beg of next 2 rows.
121 (137, 154) sts. RC 134
Cont in patt to RC 232.
Shape shoulders and neck
Place 84 (92, 101) needles at left of bed into HP, carriage at right.
Note row number on punchcard.
Working on remaining needles, cont as follows:
* Keeping pattern correct, cast off (bind off) 7 (9, 11) sts at beg of next row and 3 sts at beg of following row *.
RC 234
Rep from * to * twice more, RC 238
Cast off (bind off) remaining 7 (9, 11) sts.
Push 47 (47, 48) sts at centre of bed into WP.
Using waste yarn, knit 6 rows and release from machine.
Lock punchcard on row number previously noted and set pattern in memory.
Carriage at right.
Release card and patt 1 row.
* Keeping pattern correct, cast off (bind off) 7 (9, 11) sts at beg of next row and 3 sts at beg of following row *.
RC 235
Rep from * to * twice more. RC 239
Cast off (bind off) remaining 7 (9, 11) sts.

FRONT
Work as given for back until RC 196. Carriage at right.
Shape neck
Place 69 (77, 86) needles at left of bed into HP, carriage at right.
Note row number on punchcard.
Working on remaining 52 (60, 68) needles, cont as follows:
Keeping pattern correct, work 1 row, then cast off (bind off) 4 sts at beg of next row, 3 sts on foll 2 alt rows and 2 sts on foll 5 alt rows. 32 (40, 48) sts. RC 212
Dec 1 st at neck edge on every foll 4th row 4 times.
28 (36, 44) sts. RC 228
Work 4 rows pattern. RC 232
Shape shoulder
Cast off (bind off) 7 (9, 11) sts at beg of next and foll 2 alt rows. RC 237
Work 1 row, then cast off (bind off) remaining 7 (9, 11) sts.

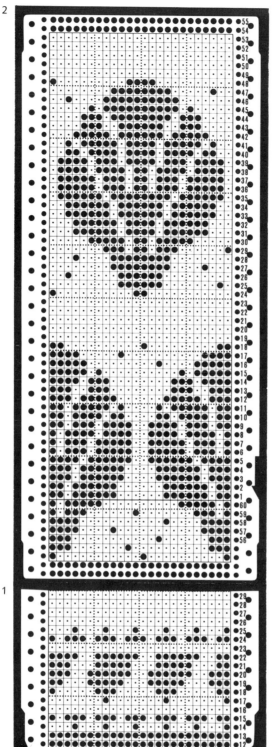

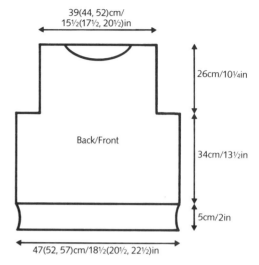

39(44, 52)cm/
15½(17½, 20½)in

Back/Front

26cm/10¼in

34cm/13½in

5cm/2in

47(52, 57)cm/18½(20½, 22½)in

58cm/23in

Sleeves

45cm/17¼in

6cm/2½in

Push 17 (17, 18) sts at centre of bed into WP.
Using waste yarn, knit 6 rows and release from machine.
Lock punchcard on row number previously noted and
set pattern in memory. RC 196.
Carriage at right.
Release card and patt 2 rows.
Keeping pattern correct, cast off (bind off) 4 sts at beg of
next row, 3 sts on foll 2 alt rows and 2 sts on foll 5 alt
rows. 32 (40, 48) sts. RC 213
Dec 1 st at neck edge on every foll 4th row 4 times.
28 (36, 44) sts. RC 229
Work 4 rows pattern. RC 233
Shape shoulder
Cast off (bind off) 7 (9, 11) sts at beg of next and foll 2
alt rows. RC 238

Work 1 row, then cast off (bind off) remaining 7 (9, 11)
sts.

SLEEVES
Bring forward 76 needles on each bed to WP. Arrange
needles for 1 × 1 rib.
Using white cast on, ending with carriage at right.
MT−2, knit 28 rows.
Insert punchcard and lock on first row of pattern.
Set patt into memory. RC 000.
MT. Working patt sequence as given in chart, inc 1 st
each end of every row until there are 96 sts. RC 10.
Keeping patt correct, inc 1 st each end of every alt row
until there are 156 sts. RC 70.
Inc 1 st each end of every foll 4th row until there are 180
sts. RC 118.
Then knit straight to RC 170, so ending with 5 rows
white.
Insert punchcard 1 and work first 4 rows of patt.
Using white only, knit 2 rows. RC 176.
Cast off (bind off) loosely.

NECKBAND
Bring forward 146 (146, 148) needles on each bed to
WP. Arrange needles for 1 × 1 rib.
Using white cast on, ending with carriage at right.
MT−3, knit 21 rows. Carriage at left.
Transfer all sts to main bed.
With WS of back facing, pick up 53 (53, 54) sts across
back neck and place on to 53 (53, 54) needles of
neckband, placing sts over top of neckband sts. With WS
of front facing, pic up 38 sts down first side of neck and
place on to next 38 needles of neckband, hook 17 (17,
18) sts from waste yarn at centre front on to needles,
then pick up 38 sts up second side of neck and hook on
to needles. 146 (146, 148) sts.
MT + 1. Knit 1 row.
Cast off (bind off) loosely.

Left: A little wavy pattern borders the cuffs and welt of Carrie White's Pastel Shells Sweater.

TO MAKE UP

With RS of back facing, replace sts of both shoulders on to needles and remove waste yarn. Push sts back behind latches.

With WS of front facing, place sts of both shoulders on to same needles holding sts of back shoulders, leaving the sts in the hooks, then remove waste yarn.

Carefully push back each needle, so pulling sts of front shoulders through sts of back shoulders. Using white, cast off (bind off) each set of shoulder sts.

Join shoulder and neckband seams.

Fold neckband in half to WS and slipstitch down. Fold sleeves in half lengthwise, then placing folds to shoulder seams, sew into position. Join side and sleeve seams.

CARRIE WHITE

SERGEANT'S STRIPES

Right: The beautiful subtle colours that form the Sergeant's Stripes on the yoke are continued in the main pattern on the body of this cardigan.

MATERIALS
Rowan Botany 4 ply
350 (375, 400) g/12 (13, 14) oz in black (62)
25 (50, 75) g/1 (2, 3) oz in brick (77)
25 (50, 75) g/1 (2, 3) oz in lupin (501)
25 (50, 75) g/1 (2, 3) oz in bracken (603)
25 (50, 75) g/1 (2, 3) oz in burgundy (602)
Rowan Grainy Silks
100 (100, 100) g/4 (4, 4) oz in blackcurrant (812)
50 (50, 100) g/2 (2, 4) oz in petrol (810)
Rowan Light Tweed
50 (50, 50) g/2 (2, 2) oz in scoured (201)
50 (50, 75) g/2 (2, 3) oz in autumn (205)
50 (50, 75) g/2 (2, 3) oz in lakeland (222)
50 (50, 75) g/2 (2, 3) oz in pebble (203)
Rowan Fine Cotton Chenille
25 (25, 50) g/1 (1, 2) oz in mole (380)
7 buttons

MEASUREMENTS
To fit bust 81–86 (91–97, 102–107) cm/32–34 (36–38, 40–42) in
Actual size
Bust 92 (102, 112) cm/36 (40, 44) in
Length 67cm/26½in
Sleeve seam 55cm/21½in

TENSION
30 sts and 38 rows to 10cm/4in worked over Fair Isle with TD at approx 8

MACHINE
Any Brother standard gauge electronic or punchcard machine with ribbing attachment or equivalent
(If ribbing attachment not available see Alternative methods of ribbing in techniques – p.123)

PATTERN SEQUENCE FOR BACK, FRONT AND SLEEVES

ROWS	PATTERN SETTING	COLOUR IN FEEDER A	COLOUR IN FEEDER B	ROWS	PATTERN SETTING	COLOUR IN FEEDER A	COLOUR IN FEEDER B
Punchcard 1 (border pattern)				45–58	Fair Isle	black	blackcurrant
(Reverse punchcard on right front and right sleeve)				59–64	plain	black	
				65–78	Fair Isle	black	autumn
1	plain	black		79–84	plain	black	
2–3	''	blackcurrant		85–98	Fair Isle	black	petrol
4–5	''	lakeland		99–104	plain	black	
	''			105–118	Fair Isle	black	blackcurrant
Release card				119–124	plain	black	
6–8	Fair Isle	scoured	brick	125–138	Fair Isle	black	autumn
9	plain	blackcurrant		139–144	plain	black	
10	''	lupin		145–158	Fair Isle	black	petrol
11	''	blackcurrant		159–164	plain	black	
12–14	Fair Isle	scoured	brick	Insert punchcard 3			
15–16	plain	lakeland		(Reverse punchcard on right sleeve)			
17–18	''	blackcurrant		Lock on row 1			
Insert punchcard 2 (joined into a circle)				165–166	plain		blackcurrant
lock on row 1				Release card			
19–24	plain	black		167–174	Fair Isle	scoured	brick
Release card				175–176	plain	blackcurrant	
25–38	Fair Isle	black	petrol	177–178	plain	black	
39–44	plain	black					

BACK
Bring forward 138 (152, 168) needles on each bed to WP. Arrange needles for 2 × 2 rib.
Using petrol cast on, ending with carriage at right.
RC 000. MT−3, change to blackcurrant and knit 2 rows.
Change to black and knit to RC 30.
Insert punchcard and lock on first row of pattern.
Set patt into memory. RC 000.
MT. Working patt sequence as given in chart, knit to RC 60.
Divide for yoke   Note row on punchcard.
Place 69 (76, 84) needles at left into HP.
Working on sts at right and keeping patt sequence correct, dec 1 st at centre front on next 5 rows. Patt 1 row. Rep the last 6 rows to RC 132. 9 (16, 24) sts.
Cast off (bind off).
Return rem sts to WP. Reset RC 000 and punchcard to row previously noted, then complete to match first side.

RIGHT FRONT
Cast on 69 (76, 84) sts.
Work as given for back to RC 60.
Shape for yoke
Dec 1 st at left on next 5 rows.
Patt 1 row.
Rep last 6 rows until RC 132. 9 (16, 24) sts.
Cast off (bind off).

LEFT FRONT
Work as given for right front, reversing all shaping.

LEFT BACK YOKE
Bring forward 77 needles (60 at left, 17 at right of centre).
Using bracken, cast on using the closed edge method.
Insert punchcard 4 and lock on first row of patt.
Set patt into memory. RC 000.
MT. Working in sequence as given for in chart for yoke,

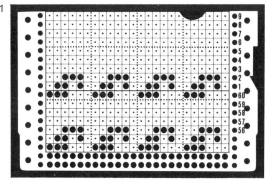

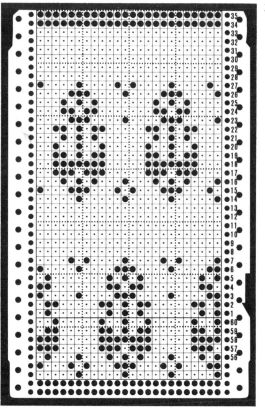

inc 1 st at right and dec 1 st at left on every row, except for rows set to slip, until RC 88.
Still omitting rows set to slip and continuing to dec 1 st at left edge on every row, dec 1 st at right on next and every foll 4th row until RC 133. 32 sts.
Still omitting rows set to slip and continuing to dec 1 st at left edge on every row, dec 1 st at right on every foll alt row until 2 sts rem. RC 156.
Cast off (bind off).

RIGHT BACK YOKE
Bring forward 77 needles (17 at left, 60 at right of centre).
Work as given for left back yoke, reversing all shaping.

RIGHT FRONT YOKE
Work as given for left back yoke to RC 132.
Cast off (bind off).

LEFT FRONT YOKE
Bring forward 77 needles (17 at left, 60 at right of centre).
Work as given for left back yoke, reversing all shaping, to RC 132.
Cast off (bind off).

SLEEVES
Bring forward 68 needles on each bed to WP. Arrange needles for 2 × 2 rib.

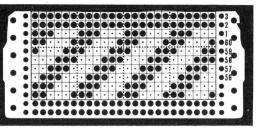

PATTERN SEQUENCE FOR YOKES

ROWS	PATTERN SETTING	COLOUR IN FEEDER A	COLOUR IN FEEDER B	ROWS	PATTERN SETTING	COLOUR IN FEEDER A	COLOUR IN FEEDER B
1–2	plain	bracken		38	slip	(empty)	
Insert punchcard 4 (joined into a circle)				39	Fair Isle	pebble	blackcurrant
				40–41	plain	pebble	
3–4	plain	bracken		42	plain	blackcurrant	
5–6	Fair Isle	bracken	black	43–44	plain	petrol	
7	slip	scoured		45–46	Fair Isle	petrol	black
8	slip	(empty)		47	slip	scoured	
9	Fair Isle	bracken	black	48	slip	(empty)	
10–11	plain	bracken		49	Fair Isle	petrol	black
12	plain	black		50–51	plain	petrol	
13–14	plain	lakeland		52	plain	black	
15–16	Fair Isle	lakeland	blackcurrant	53–54	plain	burgundy	
17	slip	scoured		55–56	Fair Isle	burgundy	black
18	slip	(empty)		57	slip	scoured	
19	Fair Isle	lakeland	blackcurrant	58	slip	(empty)	
20–21	plain	lakeland		59	Fair Isle	burgundy	black
22	plain	lupin		60–61	plain	burgundy	
23–24	plain	blackcurrant		62	plain	black	
25–26	Fair Isle	blackcurrant	black	63–64	plain	mole	
27	slip	scoured		65–66	Fair Isle	mole	blackcurrant
28	slip	(empty)		67	slip	scoured	
29	Fair Isle	blackcurrant	black	68	slip	(empty)	
30–31	plain	blackcurrant		69	Fair Isle	mole	blackcurrant
32	plain	black		70–71	plain	mole	
33–34	plain	pebble		72	plain	blackcurrant	
35–36	Fair Isle	pebble	blackcurrant	Repeat from row 3			
37	slip	scoured					

3

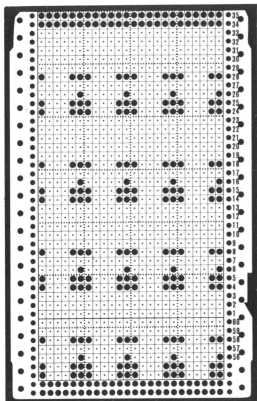

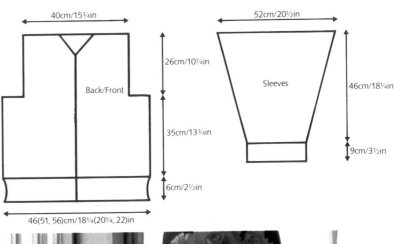

40cm/15¾in

Back/Front

26cm/10¼in

35cm/13¾in

6cm/2½in

46(51, 56)cm/18¼(20¼, 22)in

52cm/20½in

Sleeves

46cm/18¼in

9cm/3½in

Using petrol cast on, ending with carriage at right.
RC 000. MT−3, change to blackcurrant and knit 2 rows.
Change to black and knit to RC 44.
Work 6 rows waste yarn and release work from
machine.
Bring forward 88 needles on main bed to WP.
Carriage at right.
With WS of work facing, hook sts from last row worked
in black evenly over the needles, increasing sts as
necessary along the bed.
Insert punchcard and lock on first row of pattern.
Set patt into memory. RC 000.
MT. Working patt sequence as given in chart for sleeves,
inc 1 st each end of every 3rd row until there are 176 sts.
Knit straight to RC 178.
Cast off (bind off) loosely.

NECKBAND
Join centre back yoke and shoulder seams.
Bring forward 150 needles on each bed to WP. Arrange
needles for 2 × 2 rib.
Using petrol cast on, ending with carriage at right.
RC 000. MT−3, change to blackcurrant and knit 2 rows.
Change to black and knit to RC 7.
Carriage at left.
Transfer all sts to main bed.
With WS of work facing, pick up 150 sts evenly round
neck and place on to needles holding neckband sts.
MT + 1. Knit 1 row.
Cast off (bind off) loosely.

BUTTON BORDER
Sew back and front yokes into place to shaped edges of
back and fronts.
Bring forward 184 needles on each bed to WP. Arrange
needles for 2 × 2 rib.
Using petrol cast on, ending with carriage at right.
RC 000. MT−3, change to blackcurrant and knit 2 rows.
Change to black and knit to RC 7.
Carriage at left.
Transfer all sts to main bed.
With WS of work facing, pick up 184 sts evenly along
left front edge and place on to needles holding button
border sts.
MT + 1. Knit 1 row.
Cast off (bind off) loosely.

BUTTONHOLE BORDER
Work as given for button border, working buttonholes
on RC 4 as follows:
Buttonhole row
Beginning as left, miss the first 4 sts, * transfer the next 2
sts on to the adjacent needles in WP, miss the next 28
needles, rep from * to end of needles.
Leave empty needles in WP.
Cont as given for button border.

TO MAKE UP
Set in sleeves, sewing row ends at top of sleeves to cast-
off sts at underarms. Join side and sleeve seams.
Join row ends at top of button and buttonhole borders,
leaving a space on right front to form the top
buttonhole. Sew on buttons.

*Above: The yoke pattern
continues down the back of
this jacket, designed by
Carrie White, to form a V
shape. All the ribbed edges
are finished with narrow
stripes, picking out colours
in the main part of the
design.*

GROTESQUE

Right: The very simple shaping and two colour pattern makes this an ideal beginner's garment.

MATERIALS
Rowan Botany 4 ply
305 (330, 355) g/11 (12, 13) oz in main colour A
Rowan Grainy Silks
215 (240, 265) g/8½ (9, 9½) oz in contrast colour B

MEASUREMENTS
To fit chest/bust 81–86 (91–97, 102–107) cm/32–34 (36–38, 40–42) in
Actual size
Chest/bust 94 (104, 114) cm/37 (41, 45) in
Length 66cm/26in
Sleeve seam 52cm/20½in

TENSION
32 sts and 38 rows to 10cm/4in worked over st st with TD at approx 8

MACHINE
Any Brother standard gauge electronic or punchcard machine with ribbing attachment or equivalent
(If ribbing attachment not available see Alternative methods of ribbing in techniques – p.123)

BACK
Bring forward 136 (150, 160) needles on each bed to WP. Arrange needles for 1 × 1 rib.
Using A cast on, ending with carriage at right.
MT–3, knit 45 rows.
Work 6 rows waste yarn and release work from machine.
Bring forward 150 (166, 178) needles on main bed to WP.

Carriage at right.
Hook sts from last row worked in A evenly over the needles, increasing sts as necessary along the bed. Insert punchcards 1, 2, 3 and 4 (joined together) and lock on first row of pattern.
RC 000. MT–1. Knit 2 rows B, 2 rows A, then 2 rows B. RC 6.
Set machine for Fair Isle. MT.
With A in feeder A and B in feeder B, knit to RC 120.
Place a marker at each side to denote depth of armholes.
Knit to RC 216.
Place a marker at the 29th st each side of centre of needlebed to denote back neck.
Cast off (bind off) all sts.

FRONT
Work as given for back until RC 190. Carriage at right.
Shape neck
Note row on punchcard.
With a spare length of yarn, cast off (bind off) centre 16 sts.
Push all needles at left of needlebed to HP.
Work on first side of neck as follows: Knit 1 row.
Cast off (bind off) 3 sts at beg of next and foll 4 alt rows and 2 sts at beg of foll 2 alt rows.

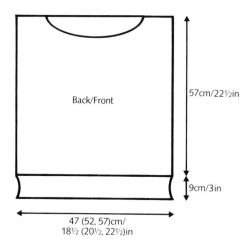

57cm/22½in

9cm/3in

Back/Front

47 (52, 57)cm/
18½ (20½, 22½)in

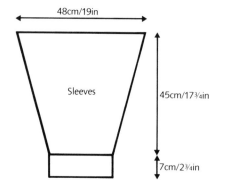

48cm/19in

Sleeves

45cm/17¾in

7cm/2¾in

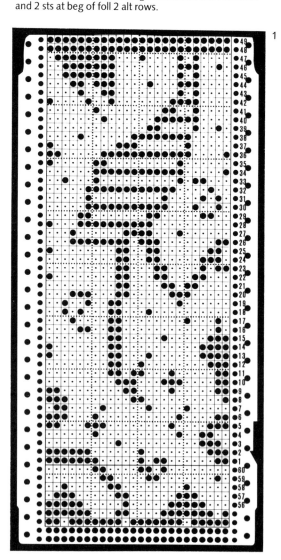

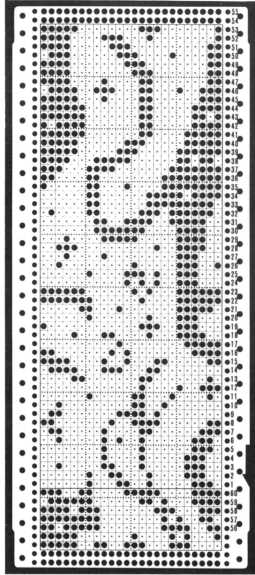

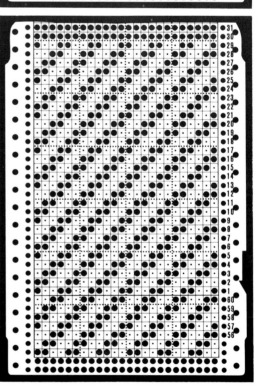

Dec 1 st at neck edge on foll 2 alt rows. 46 (54, 60) sts.
Knit straight to RC 216.
Cast off (bind off).
Return punchcard to row number previously noted.
Set patt into memory. RC 190.
Return needles at left to WP.
Complete to match first side of neck, reversing all
shaping.

SLEEVES
Bring forward 70 needles on each bed to WP. Arrange
needles for 1 × 1 rib.
Using A cast on, ending with carriage at right.
MT−3, knit 35 rows.
Work 6 rows waste yarn and release work from
machine.
Bring forward 80 needles on main bed to WP.
Hook sts from last row worked in A evenly over the
needles, increasing sts as necessary along the bed.
Carriage at right.
Insert punchcards 1, 2, 3 and 4 (joined together) and
lock on first row of pattern.
RC 000. MT−1. Knit 2 rows B, 2 rows A, then 2 rows B.
RC 6.
Set machine for Fair Isle. MT.
With A in feeder A and B in feeder B, inc 1 st each end of
every 4th row until there are 152 sts. RC 151.
Knit straight to RC 170, so ending with 2 rows B.
Set machine for plain knitting.
Knit 1 row A.
Cast off (bind off) loosely.

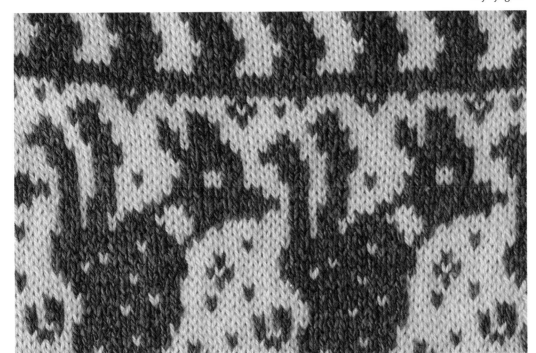

Left: Experiment with dark and light backgrounds to create a different effect.

Below: Edy Lyngaas' Grotesque Sweater is shown here knitted in different colours; being quick to knit, make several to complement your wardrobe.

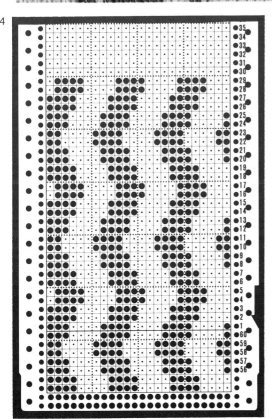

4

COLLAR
Bring forward 14 needles on main bed to WP.
With A, cast on using the closed edge method.
Insert punchcard 5 only, joining into a circle.
Set machine for Fair Isle.
RC 000. MT. With A in feeder A and B in feeder B, knit to RC 160.
Cast off (bind off).

TO MAKE UP
Join shoulder seams.
Folds sleeves in half lengthwise, then placing folds to shoulder seams, sew into position. Join side and sleeve seams. Join centre back collar seam, then sew one long edge to neck edge, allowing to roll over to right side.

EDY LYNGAAS

SETERSDAL

MATERIALS
Rowan Botany 4 ply
260 (285, 310) g/9½ (10½, 11½) oz in main colour A
Rowan Silkstones
250 (250, 300) g/9 (10, 11) oz in contrast colour B

MEASUREMENTS
To fit chest/bust 81–86 (91-97, 102–107) cm/32–34
(36–38, 40–42) in
Actual size
Chest/bust 97 (107, 117) cm/38 (42, 46) in
Length 66cm/26in
Sleeve seam 54cm/21½in

TENSION
31 sts and 36 rows to 10cm/4in worked over st st with
TD at approx 9

MACHINE
Any Brother standard gauge electronic or punchcard
machine with ribbing attachment or equivalent
(If ribbing attachment not available see Alternative
methods of ribbing in techniques – p.123)

PATTERN SEQUENCE FOR BACK, FRONT AND SLEEVES

ROWS	PATTERN SETTING	COLOUR IN FEEDER A	COLOUR IN FEEDER B
Punchcards 1, 2, 3 and 4 (joined together)			
1–end	Fair Isle	A	B

BACK
Bring forward 150 (166, 182) needles on each bed to
WP. Arrange needles for 2 × 2 rib.
Using A cast on, ending with carriage at right.
MT−4, knit 36 rows.
Transfer all sts to main bed.
Insert punchcard and lock on first row of pattern.
Set patt into memory. RC 000.
MT. Increasing 1 st each end of first row, knit 1 row in A.
RC 1.
Set machine for Fair Isle.
Working patt sequence as given in chart, knit to RC 213.
Set machine for plain knitting.
Knit 1 row A. RC 214.
Place a marker at the 29th st each side of centre of
needlebed to denote back neck.
Cast off (bind off) all sts.

FRONT
Work as given for back until RC 176. Carriage at right.
Note row on punchcard.
Shape neck
With a spare length of yarn, cast off (bind off) centre 16
sts.
Push all needles at left of needlebed to HP.
Work on first side of neck as follows:
Cast off (bind off) 3 sts at beg of next and foll alt row,
then 2 sts at beg of foll 7 alt rows.
Dec 1 st at neck edge on foll alt row. 46 (54, 62) sts.
Knit straight to RC 214.
Cast off (bind off).
Return punchcard to row number previously noted.
Set patt into memory. RC 176.
Return needles at left to WP.
Complete to match first side of neck, reversing all
shaping.

Left: Use the dark coloured yarn as either the main or contrast yarn to create the effect you require.

Above: Only two colours are used to knit Edy Lyngaas' Setersdal jersey, so it is quick and easy to make.

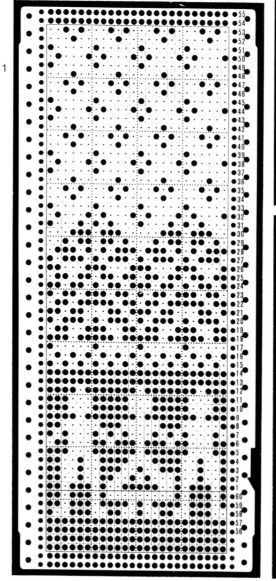

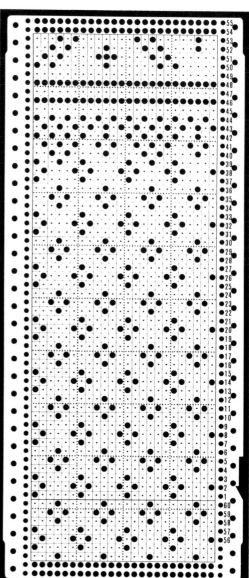

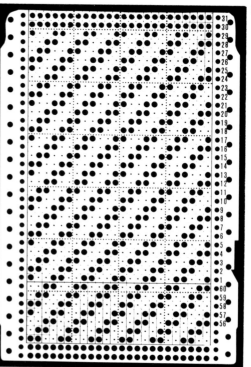

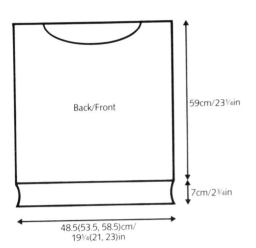

Back/Front

59cm/23¼in

7cm/2¾in

48.5(53.5, 58.5)cm/
19¼(21, 23)in

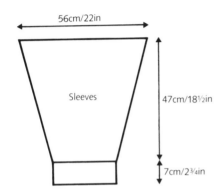

56cm/22in

Sleeves

47cm/18½in

7cm/2¾in

3

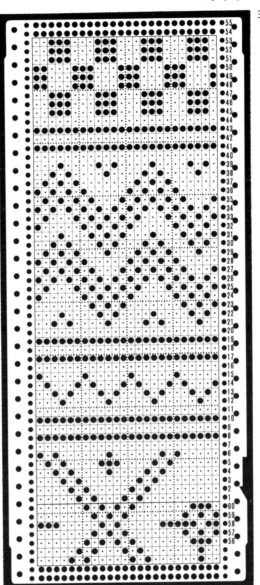

4

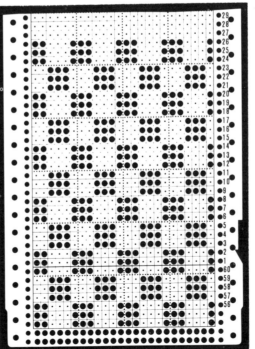

SLEEVES
Bring forward 86 needles on each bed to WP. Arrange needles for 2 × 2 rib.
Using A cast on, ending with carriage at right.
MT−4, knit 36 rows.
Work 6 rows waste yarn and release work from machine.
Bring forward 94 needles on main bed to WP.
Carriage at right.
With WS of work facing, hook sts from last row worked in A evenly over the needles, increasing sts as necessary along the bed.
Insert punchcard and lock on first row of pattern.
Set patt into memory. RC 000.
MT. Knit 1 row with A.
Set machine for Fair Isle.
Working patt sequence as given in chart, inc 1 st each end of next and every foll 4th row until there are 174 sts.
Knit straight to RC 172.
Set machine for plain knitting.
Knit 2 rows in A.
Cast off (bind off) loosely.

COLLAR
Bring forward 14 needles on main bed to WP.
With A, cast on using the closed edge method.
Insert punchcard 5 only, joining into a circle, and lock on first row of pattern.
Set patt into memory. RC 000.
MT. Set machine for Fair Isle.
With A in feeder A and B in feeder B, knit to RC 160.
Cast off (bind off).

TO MAKE UP
Join shoulder seams. Folds sleeves in half lengthwise, then placing folds to shoulder seams, sew into position.
Join side and sleeve seams. Join centre back collar seam, then sew one long edge to neck edge, allowing to roll over to right side.

MAGGIE WHITE

BLUE IKAT

Right: Diagonal lines, wavy lines and chevrons cover this jacket, knitted in many shades of cotton chenille and fine wool.

MATERIALS
Rowan Fine Fleck Tweed
250g/9oz in Royal (shade 56)
50g/2oz in Navy (shade 97)
Rowan Botany 4 ply
50g/2oz in green (shade 90)
25g/1oz in mauve (shade 126)
25g/1oz in magenta (shade 96)
25g/1oz in mustard (shade 14)
Rowan Fine Cotton Chenille
350g/13oz in ecru (shade 376)
50g/2oz in lacquer (shade 388)
50g/2oz in cyclamen (shade 385)
50g/2oz in steel (shade 382)
12 buttons

MEASUREMENTS
To fit bust 91-102cm/36–40in
Actual size
Bust 116cm/46in
Length 66cm/26in
Sleeve seam 45cm/18in

TENSION
29 sts and 43 rows to 10cm/4in worked over Fair Isle with TD at approx 7

MACHINE
Any Brother standard gauge electronic or punchcard machine or equivalent

PATTERN SEQUENCE FOR BACK AND FRONT

ROWS	PATTERN SETTING	COLOUR IN FEEDER A	COLOUR IN FEEDER B	ROWS	PATTERN SETTING	COLOUR IN FEEDER A	COLOUR IN FEEDER B
Punchcard 1				Punchcard 3 (locked on row 1)			
1–20	Fair Isle	blue	ecru	111–114	,,	navy	cyclamen
Punchcard 2				Release card			
21–26	,,	navy	lacquer	115–126	,,	green	ecru
Punchcard 3 (locked on row 1)				Lock card			
27–28	,,	green	cyclamen	127–130	,,	navy	cyclamen
Release card				Punchcard 1			
29–40	,,	ecru	steel	131–160	,,	blue	ecru
Lock card				Punchcard 2			
41–42	,,	green	cyclamen	161–166	,,	navy	purple
Punchcard 2				Punchcard 1			
43–48	,,	navy	lacquer	167–200	,,	blue	ecru
Punchcard 1				Punchcard 2			
49–70	,,	blue	ecru	201–206	,,	green	steel
Punchcard 2				Punchcard 1			
71–76	,,	green	cyclamen	207–210	,,	blue	ecru
Punchcard 1				Punchcard 2			
77–84	,,	blue	ecru	211–216	,,	magenta	mustard
Punchcard 2				Punchcard 1			
85–90	,,	navy	mustard	217–224	,,	blue	ecru
Punchard 1				Punchcard 2			
91–98	,,	blue	ecru	225–230	,,	navy	lacquer
Punchcard 2				Punchcard 1			
99–104	,,	purple	lacquer	231–234	,,	blue	ecru
Punchcard 1				Punchcard 2			
105–110	,,	blue	ecru	235–240	,,	purple	cyclamen

BACK
Bring forward 160 needles to WP.
Insert punchcard 1 and lock on first row.
Cast on with waste yarn and knit 6 rows.
RC 000. MT. Working in patt sequence as given in chart and setting each patt into memory without recording a row on the row counter, knit to RC 240.
Using waste yarn, knit 6 rows.

Release sts from machine.

LEFT FRONT
Work as given for back to RC 89.
Shape neck
Keeping patt correct, cast off (bind off) 6 sts at left at beg of next row, then dec 1 st at neck edge on next and every foll alt row to RC 110. 144 sts.

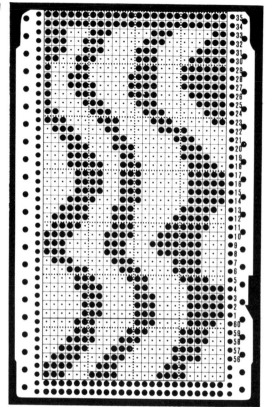

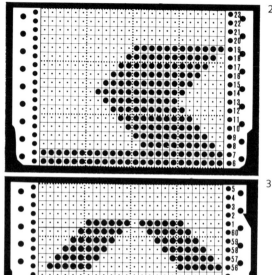

Knit straight to RC 120.
Leave punchcard 3 in and lock on row 7.
Using waste yarn, knit 6 rows.
Release sts from machine.

RIGHT FRONT
Bring forward 144 needles to WP. (80 needles at right
and 64 needles at left.)
With punchcard 3 still locked on same row, release card.

PATTERN SEQUENCE FOR LEFT SLEEVE

ROWS	PATTERN SETTING	COLOUR IN FEEDER A	COLOUR IN FEEDER B	ROWS	PATTERN SETTING	COLOUR IN FEEDER A	COLOUR IN FEEDER B
Punchcard 2				Punchcard 3 (locked on row 1)			
1–6	Fair Isle	navy	mustard	93–96	''	navy	cyclamen
Punchcard 1				Release card			
7–20	''	blue	ecru	97–108	''	green	ecru
Punchcard 2				Lock card			
21–26	''	green	cyclamen	109–112	''	navy	cyclamen
Punchcard 1				Punchcard 1			
27–40	''	blue	ecru	113–132	''	blue	ecru
Punchcard 2				Punchcard 2			
41–46	''	purple	lacquer	133–138	''	cyclamen	mustard
Punchcard 1				Punchcard 1			
47–92	''	blue	ecru	139–142	''	blue	ecru

PATTERN SEQUENCE FOR LEFT CUFF

ROWS	PATTERN SETTING	COLOUR IN FEEDER A	COLOUR IN FEEDER B	ROWS	PATTERN SETTING	COLOUR IN FEEDER A	COLOUR IN FEEDER B
Punchcard 1				Punchcard 2			
1–10	Fair Isle	blue	ecru	41–46	''	green	steel
Punchcard 2				Punchcard 1			
11–16	''	navy	lacquer	47–56	''	blue	ecru
Punchcard 1				57–99	plain	blue	
17–40	''	blue	ecru				

With green in feeder A and ecru in feeder B, set machine for Fair Isle and knit 6 rows. Set RC to 126.
Beg with row 127 and working in patt sequence from chart for back and front, knit to RC 130.
Continuing in patt, inc 1 st at right o next and every foll alt row until there are 154 sts. RC 150.
Cast on 6 sts at beg of next row, then cont in patt to RC 240.
Using waste yarn, knit 6 rows.
Release sts from machine.

LEFT SLEEVE
Bring forward 160 needles to WP.
With WS of front facing, placing 2 sts on to first needle at left of centre, pick up 81 sts from first row after waste yarn at side edge of front and place on to remaining needles at left.
With WS of back facing, placing 2 sts on to first needle at right of centre, pick up 81 sts from first row after waste yarn at side edge of back and place on to remaining needles at right.
Insert punchcard 2 and lock on first row.
Set patt into memory. RC 000.
Working in patt sequence as given in chart for left sleeve, dec 1 st each end of every 8th row until 126 sts rem.
Knit straight to RC 142.
Using waste yarn, knit 6 rows.
Remove sts from machine.

CUFF
Bring forward 63 needles to WP.
Replace sts at lower edge of sleeve on to needles, placing 2 sts on to each needle.
Remove waste yarn.
Set patt into memory. RC 000.
Working in patt sequence as given in chart for left cuff,

knit to RC 99.
Make hem by picking up loops from sts of first row and placing them on to needles.
MT + 1. Knit 1 row in blue.
Cast off (bind off) loosely.

RIGHT SLEEVE AND CUFF
Bring forward 160 needles to WP.
Placing 2 sts on to first needle each side of centre, and working patt sequence as given in charts for right sleeve and right cuff, work as given for left sleeve and cuff.

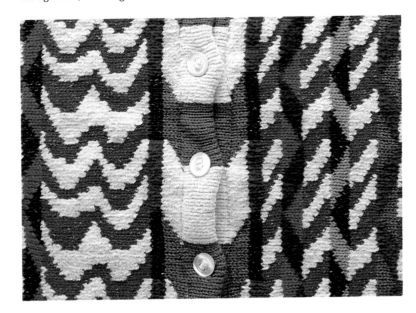

Below: The fronts and borders have been cleverly designed so that the pattern matches exactly when the two fronts are buttoned up.

PATTERN SEQUENCE FOR RIGHT SLEEVE

ROWS	PATTERN SETTING	COLOUR IN FEEDER A	COLOUR IN FEEDER B	ROWS	PATTERN SETTING	COLOUR IN FEEDER A	COLOUR IN FEEDER B
Punchcard 1				Punchcard 2			
1–30	Fair Isle	blue	ecru	101–106	''	purple	lacquer
Punchcard 3 (locked on row 1)				Punchcard 1			
31–34	''	green	cyclamen	107–112	''	blue	ecru
Release card				Punchcard 2			
35–46	''	ecru	steel	113–118	''	navy	mustard
Lock card				Punchcard 1			
47–50	''	green	cyclamen	119–126	''	blue	ecru
Punchcard 1				Punchcard 2			
51–60	''	blue	ecru	127–132	''	green	cyclamen
Punchcard 2				Punchcard 1			
61–66	''	magenta	mustard	133–142	''	blue	ecru
Punchcard 1							
67–100	''	blue	ecru				

PATTERN SEQUENCE FOR RIGHT CUFF

ROWS	PATTERN SETTING	COLOUR IN FEEDER A	COLOUR IN FEEDER B	ROWS	PATTERN SETTING	COLOUR IN FEEDER A	COLOUR IN FEEDER B
Punchcard 1				Punchcard 1			
1–30	Fair Isle	blue	ecru	37–44	''	blue	ecru
Punchcard 2				Punchcard 2			
31–36	''	purple	mustard	45–50	''	green	cyclamen
				51–99	plain	blue	

PATTERN SEQUENCE FOR WELTS

ROWS	PATTERN SETTING	COLOUR IN FEEDER A	COLOUR IN FEEDER B	ROWS	PATTERN SETTING	COLOUR IN FEEDER A	COLOUR IN FEEDER B
Punchcard 1				**Punchcard 2**			
1–30	Fair Isle	blue	ecru	41–46	,,	green	cyclamen
Punchcard 2				**Punchcard 1**			
31–36	,,	navy	lacquer	47–54	,,	blue	ecru
Punchcard 1				55–59	plain	blue	
37–40	,,	blue	ecru				

WELTS

Bring forward 130 needles to WP.
With WS facing, pick up 130 sts from lower edge of back and place on to needles.
Insert punchcard 1 and lock on first row of patt.
Set patt into memory. RC 000.
MT. Working in patt sequence as given in chart for welts, knit to RC 99.
Make hem by picking up loops of first row of patt and placing on to needles.
MT + 1. Knit 1 row blue.
Cast off (bind off) loosely.
Repeat for front welt, except only pick up 65 sts along lower edge of each front.

BUTTON BORDER

Bring forward 174 needles. (88 at left of centre and 86 at right.)
Insert punchcard 3 and lock on row 6 of patt.
Set machine for Fair Isle.
With green in feeder A and ecru in feeder B, knit 12 rows.

Set machine for plain knitting.
Knit 11 rows ecru.
Make hem by picking up loops of first row and placing on to needles.
MT + 1. Knit 1 row.
Cast off loosely.

BUTTONHOLE BORDER

Work as given for button border, bringing forward 86 needles at left and 88 needles at right, and working buttonholes on row 8 and 16 as follows:
Buttonhole row
Miss first 6 needles at left, * using a short length of yarn, cast off 3 sts, then using the same length of yarn, cast on aain over these 3 sts *, miss next 7 sts, rep from * to *, miss next 7 sts, rep from * to *, [miss next 14 sts, rep from * to *] 8 times, miss last 9 sts.

NECKBAND

Join shoulder seams.
Bring forward 122 needles to WP.
Picking up 122 sts evenly round neck and placing on to needles, work as given for button border working a buttonhole on rows 8 and 16 as follows:
Buttonhole row
Miss first 3 needles at left, rep from * to * as given in butonhole border, miss rem sts.

TO MAKE UP

With RS of back facing, replace sts of side seam on to needles and remove waste yarn. Push sts back behind latches.
With WS of front facing, place sts of corresponding seam on to same needles holding sts of back, leaving the sts in the hooks, then remove waste yarn.
Carefully push back each needle, so pulling sts of front through sts of back.
Using ecru, cast off (bind off) sts.
Repeat on 2nd side seam.
Join sleeve seams. Join welt seams. Sew on buttons.

Below: The Blue Ikat jacket is worked sideways, so the stitches run horizontally across the back and fronts of this design.

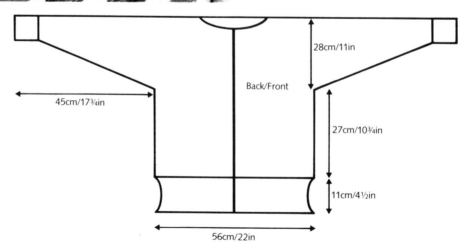

MAGGIE WHITE

SPEARMINT SWEATER

MATERIALS
Rowan Light Tweed
300g/11oz in scoured (shade 201)
Rowan Botany 4 ply
225g/9oz in red (shade 44)
100g/4oz in magenta (shade 96)
25g/1oz in yellow (shade 12)
25g/1oz in mauve (shade 126)
25g/1oz in kelly green (shade 124)
25g/1oz in bright green (shade 34)
25g/1oz in duck egg (125)
50g/2oz in pink (shade 621)
Rowan Fine Cotton Chenille
50g/2oz in purple (shade 384)
4 buttons

MEASUREMENTS
To fit bust 91–102cm/36–40in
Actual size
Bust 116cm/46in
Length 63cm/25in
Sleeve seam 45cm/18in

TENSION
31 sts and 41 rows to 10cm/4in worked over Fair Isle
with TD at approx 7

MACHINE
Any Brother standard gauge electronic or punchcard
machine or equivalent

PATTERN SEQUENCE FOR BACK AND FRONT

ROWS	PATTERN SETTING	COLOUR IN FEEDER A	COLOUR IN FEEDER B	ROWS	PATTERN SETTING	COLOUR IN FEEDER A	COLOUR IN FEEDER B
Punchcard 1 (joined into a circle)				Insert punchcard 1 (joined into a circle)			
Release card				Set patt into memory			
1–20	Fair Isle	red	white	113–140	Fair Isle	red	white
Lock card				141–142	''	red	bright green
21–24	''	white	mauve	143–146	''	red	white
Release card				147–148	''	red	bright green
25–40	''	red	white	149–150	''	red	white
Lock card				151–152	''	red	bright green
41–44	''	white	yellow	153–160	''	red	white
Release card				Lock card			
46–56	''	magenta	white	161–164	''	white	magenta
57–64	''	red	white	Release card			
65–66	''	red	kelly green	165–178	''	red	white
67–68	''	red	white	179–180	''	purple	white
69–70	''	magenta	white	181–184	''	magenta	white
71–72	''	magenta	kelly green	185–188	''	purple	white
73–90	''	magenta	white	189–202	''	red	white
Lock card				Lock card			
91–94	''	white	magenta	203–206	''	white	kelly green
Release card				Release card			
95–108	''	red	white	207–216	''	red	white
Insert punchcard 2				217–230	''	magenta	white
Set patt into memory				231–232	''	magenta	pink
109–112	Fair Isle	magenta	yellow	233–234	''	magenta	white
				235–236	''	magenta	duck egg
				237–240	''	magenta	white

BACK
Bring forward 160 needles to WP.
Insert punchcard 1 (joined into a circle) and lock on first
row.
Cast on with waste yarn and knit 6 rows.
RC 000. MT. Working in patt sequence as given in chart,
knit to RC 240.
Using waste yarn, knit 6 rows.
Release sts from machine.

FRONT
Work as given for back to RC 89.
Shape neck
Keeping patt correct, cast off (bind off) 6 sts at left at
beg of next row, then dec 1 st at neck edge on next and
every foll alt row to RC 110.
Knit straight to RC 130.
Inc 1 st at neck edge on next and every foll alt row to RC
151.
Cast on 6 sts at left at beg of next row.
160 sts. RC 152.
Cont in patt to RC 240.
Using waste yarn, knit 6 rows.
Release sts from machine.

LEFT SHOULDER BUTTONHOLE BORDER
Bring forward 60 needles to WP.
With WS of left front facing, pick up 60 sts along left
shoulder edge and place on to needles.
MT–1, RC 000. Using red, knit 5 rows.

Maggie White

Right: Seaside rock colours zigzag and stripe across a white background on this sideways knitted sweater.

Make buttonholes
Counting from left, miss first 10 sts, * using a short length of yarn, cast off (bind off) by hand the next 3 sts, then using the same piece of yarn, cast on again over these 3 needles *, [miss next 10 sts, rep from * to *] 3 times, miss last 8 sts.
Knit 1 row.
MT−2. Knit to RC 11.
MT + 1. Knit 1 row.
MT−2. Knit to RC 17.
MT−1. Knit 1 row.
Rep the buttonhole row once more, then knit to RC 23.
Make hem by picking up loops of first row and placing on to needles.
MT + 1. Knit 1 row.
Cast off (bind off) loosely.

LEFT SHOULDER BUTTON BORDER
Bring forward 60 needles to WP.
With WS facing, pick up sts along corresponding row ends of left shoulder on back and work as given for buttonhole border, omitting the buttonholes.

LEFT SLEEVE
Bring forward 160 needles to WP.
With WS of front facing, pick up 6 sts across row ends of buttonhole border and place on to 6 needles at centre of bed. (3 sts each side of 0.)
Pick up 77 sts from first row after waste yarn at side edge of front and place on to remaining needles at left.
With WS of back facing, pick up 6 sts across row ends of button border and place over top of 6 sts of buttonhole border.
Pick up 77 sts from first row after waste yarn at side edge of back and place on to remaining needles at right.
Insert punchcard 1 (joined into a circle) and lock on first row.
Set patt into memory. RC 000.
Working in patt sequence as given in chart for left

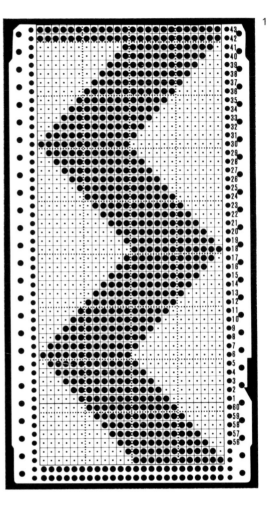

1

PATTERN SEQUENCE FOR LEFT SLEEVE

ROWS	PATTERN SETTING	COLOUR IN FEEDER A	COLOUR IN FEEDER B	ROWS	PATTERN SETTING	COLOUR IN FEEDER A	COLOUR IN FEEDER B
Punchcard 1 (joined into a circle)				55–66	′′	red	white
				67–78	′′	magenta	white
Lock card				79–88	′′	red	white
1–4	Fair Isle	magenta	mauve	89–92	′′	red	yellow
				93–100	′′	red magenta	white
Release card							
5–34	′′	red	white	101–114	′′	magenta	white
35–38	′′	red	bright green	115–116	′′	red	white
39–42	′′	red	white	117–118	′′	red	mauve
43–44	′′	red	bright green	119–120	′′	red	white
45–46	′′	red	duck egg	121–122	′′	red	mauve
47–50	′′	red	white	123–126	′′	red	white
51–54	′′	red	pink	127–140	′′	magenta	white

PATTERN SEQUENCE FOR LEFT CUFF

ROWS	PATTERN SETTING	COLOUR IN FEEDER A	COLOUR IN FEEDER B	ROWS	PATTERN SETTING	COLOUR IN FEEDER A	COLOUR IN FEEDER B
Punchcard 1 (joined into a circle)				25–28	′′	magenta	white
Release card				29–30	′′	magenta	kelly green
1-12	Fair Isle	magenta	white	31–36	′′	magenta	white
13–16	′′	red	white	37–44	′′	red	white
17–18	′′	red	kelly green	45–48	′′	mauve	red
19–22	′′	red	white	49–50	′′	red	white
23–24	′′	red	kelly green	51–99	plain	red	

2

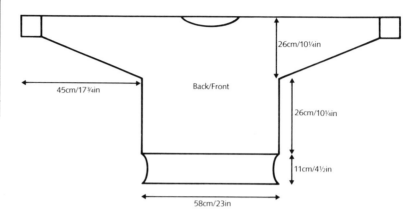

26cm/10¼in

45cm/17¾in

Back/Front

26cm/10¼in

11cm/4½in

58cm/23in

sleeve, dec 1 st each end of every 8th row until 126 sts rem.
Knit straight to RC 140.
Using waste yarn, knit 6 rows.
Remove sts from machine.

CUFF
Bring forward 63 needles to WP.
Replace sts at lower edge of sleeve on to needles, placing 2 sts on to each needle.
Remove waste yarn.
Set patt into memory. RC 000. MT.
Working in patt sequence as given in chart for left cuff,

knit to RC 99.
Make hem by picking up loops from sts of first row and placing them on to needles.
MT + 1. Knit 1 row in red.
Cast off (bind off) loosely.

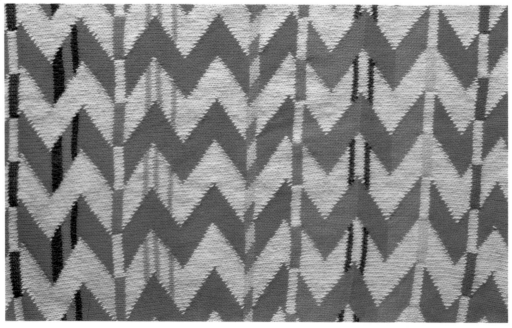

Top Left: The neckband and shoulder opening are all worked in plain stocking stitch.

Bottom Left: Close detail of the brilliant colours of this design.

PATTERN SEQUENCE FOR RIGHT SLEEVE

ROWS	PATTERN SETTING	COLOUR IN FEEDER A	COLOUR IN FEEDER B	ROWS	PATTERN SETTING	COLOUR IN FEEDER A	COLOUR IN FEEDER B
Punchcard 1 (joined into a circle)							
Release card				81–84	,,	red	white
				85–86	,,	red	mauve
1–2	Fair Isle	yellow	bright green	87–98	,,	red	white
3–14	,,	magenta	white	99–102	,,	magenta	white
15–26	,,	red	white	103–106	,,	magenta	yellow
27–34	,,	magenta	white	107–120	,,	magenta	white
35–38	,,	magenta	mauve	121–122	,,	red	white
39–60	,,	red	white	123–124	,,	red	kelly green
61–62	,,	kelly green	white	125–126	,,	red	white
63–66	,,	magenta	white	127–128	,,	red	kelly green
67–72	,,	kelly green	white	129–130	,,	red	white
73–78	,,	red	white	131–132	,,	red	kelly green
79–80	,,	red	mauve	133–140	,,	magenta	white

PATTERN SEQUENCE FOR RIGHT CUFF

ROWS	PATTERN SETTING	COLOUR IN FEEDER A	COLOUR IN FEEDER B	ROWS	PATTERN SETTING	COLOUR IN FEEDER A	COLOUR IN FEEDER B
Punchcard (joined into a circle)				23–24	,,	magenta	mauve
Release card				25–26	,,	magenta	white
				27–40	,,	red	white
1–12	Fair Isle	magenta	white	41–44	,,	red	mauve
13–14	,,	magenta	mauve	45–46	,,	red	white
15–22	,,	magenta	white	47–99	plain	red	

PATTERN SEQUENCE FOR WELTS

ROWS	PATTERN SETTING	COLOUR IN FEEDER A	COLOUR IN FEEDER B	ROWS	PATTERN SETTING	COLOUR IN FEEDER A	COLOUR IN FEEDER B
Punchcard 1 (joined into a circle)				25–28	,,	red	white
Release card				29–30	,,	red	yellow
				31–36	,,	red	white
1–12	Fair Isle	red	white	37–40	,,	magenta	white
13–16	,,	magenta	white	41–42	,,	magenta	bright green
17–18	,,	magenta	mauve	43–52	,,	magenta	white
19–24	,,	magenta	white	53–99	plain	red	

RIGHT SLEEVE AND CUFF
Bring forward 160 needles to WP.
Placing 2 sts on to first needle each side of centre, and working patt sequence as given in charts for right sleeve and right cuff, work as given for left sleeve and cuff.

WELTS
Bring forward 130 needles to WP.
With WS facing, pick up 130 sts from lower edge of back and place on to needles.
Insert punchcard 1 (joined into a circle) and lock on first row of patt.
Set patt into memory. RC 000.
MT. Working in patt sequence as given in chart for welts, knit to RC 99.
Make hem by picking up loops of first row of patt and placing on to needles.
MT + 1. Knit 1 row red.
Cast off (bind off) loosely.
Repeat for front welt.

NECKBAND
Join right shoulder seam.
Bring forward 122 needles to WP.

Pick up 122 sts evenly round neck and place on to needles.
RC 000. MT−1. Using red, knit 5 rows.
MT−2. Knit 4 rows.
MT + 2. Knit 1 row.
MT−2. Knit 4 rows.
MT−1. Knit to RC 19.
Make hem by picking up loops of first row and placing on to needles.
MT + 1. Knit 1 row.
Cast off (bind off) loosely.

TO MAKE UP
With RS of back facing, replace sts of side seam on to needles and remove waste yarn. Push sts back behind latches.
With WS of front facing, place sts of corresponding seam on to same needles holding sts of back, leaving the sts in the hooks, then remove waste yarn.
Carefully push back each needle, so pulling sts of front through sts of back.
Using white, cast off (bind off) sts.
Repeat on 2nd side seam.
Join sleeve seams. Join welt seams. Sew on buttons.

SARAH DALLAS

DOT 'N' ZIGZAG

Right: The back and skirt of this suit are plain navy with a narrow red and green border.

MATERIALS
Rowan Lightweight Double Knitting
900 (950, 1000) g/32 (33, 35) oz in navy (shade 97)
220 (245, 270) g/8½ (9, 9½) oz in green (shade 91)
50g/2oz in red (shade 46)
Waist length of elastic

MEASUREMENTS
To fit bust 81–86 (91-97, 102–107) cm/32–34 (36–38, 40–42) in
Actual size
Bust 92 (102, 112) cm/36 (40, 44) in
Length 68cm/27in

Sleeve seam 49cm/19½in
Hips 92 (102, 112) cm/36 (40, 44) in
Skirt length 46cm/18in

TENSION
29 sts and 36 rows to 10cm/4in worked over st st with TD at approx 9

MACHINE
Any Brother standard gauge electronic or punchcard machine with ribbing attachment or equivalent (If ribbing attachment not available see Alternative methods of ribbing in techniques – p.123)

PATTERN SEQUENCE FOR BORDER

ROWS	PATTERN SETTING	COLOUR IN FEEDER A	COLOUR IN FEEDER B	ROWS	PATTERN SETTING	COLOUR IN FEEDER A	COLOUR IN FEEDER B
Punchcard 1							
1	plain	green		6–12	Fair Isle	navy	red
2	,,	navy		13–14	plain	navy	
3	,,	green		15	,,	green	
4–5	,,	navy		16	,,	navy	
Release card				17	,,	green	

TUNIC BACK
Bring forward 133 (147, 163) needles on each bed to WP. Arrange needles for 1 × 1 rib.
Using red cast on, ending with carriage at right.
Cut off red and join on navy.
MT−4, knit 30 rows.
Transfer all sts to main bed.
Insert punchcard 1 and lock on first row of pattern.
Set patt into memory. RC 000.
MT. Knit 2 rows.
Working patt sequence as given in chart for border, knit to RC 19
Continuing in navy only, knit to RC 136.
Place a marker at each end of last row to denote the beginning of armholes.
Knit to RC 218.
Shape shoulders
Winding yarn round first needle in HP at beg of every row, place 13 needles at opposite end to carriage into HP at beg of next 2 rows, then place 10 (12, 14) needles into HP at beg of foll 6 rows.
Using waste yarn, knit 6 rows over rem 47 (49, 53) needles. Release sts from machine.
Return 43 (49, 55) needles at left into WP. Using waste yarn, knit 6 rows. Release sts from machine.
Return rem sts to WP. Using waste yarn, knit 6 rows. Release sts from machine.

TUNIC FRONT
Cast on and work 30 rows rib as given for back.
Transfer all sts to main bed.
Insert punchcard 2 (joined into a circle) and lock on first row of pattern.
Set patt into memory. RC 000.
MT. Knit 2 rows.
Set machine for Fair Isle. MT + 1.
Working with navy in feeder A and green in feeder B throughout, knit to RC 136.
Place a marker at each end of last row to denote the beginning of armholes.

Continuing in patt, knit to RC 208.
Shape neck
Note row on punchcard.
Place centre 23 (25, 29) needles into HP.
Push all needles at left of needlebed to HP.
Work on first side of neck as follows:
Dec 1st at neck edge on next 8 rows.
Knit 1 row. RC 217.
Winding yarn round first needle in HP, place 13 sts at opposite end to carriage into HP on next row.
Dec 1 st at neck edge on next row. RC 219.
Winding yarn round first needle in HP, place 10 (12, 14) sts at opposite end to carriage into HP on next row.
Dec 1 st at neck edge on next row. RC 221.
Winding yarn round first needle in HP, place 10 (12, 14) sts at opposite end to carriage into HP on next row.
Dec 1 st at neck edge on next row. RC 223.
Knit 1 row, then dec 1 st at neck edge on next row.
RC 225.
Using waste yarn, knit 6 rows. Release sts from machine.
Return 23 (25, 29) centre sts to WP.
Using waste yarn, knit 6 rows. Release sts from machine.
Return punchcard to row number previously noted.
Set patt into memory. RC 208.
Return needles at left to WP.
Complete to match first side of neck, reversing all shaping.

TUNIC SLEEVES
Bring forward 80 needles on each bed to WP. Arrange needles for 1 × 1 rib.
Cast on and work 30 rows rib as given for back.
Transfer all sts to main bed.
Insert punchcard 3 (joined into a circle) and lock on first row of pattern.
Set patt into memory. RC 000.
MT. Knit 2 rows.
Set machine for Fair Isle. MT + 1.
Working with navy in feeder A and green in feeder B throughout, inc 1 st each end of every 4th row until

Sarah Dallas

there are 150 sts.
Knit straight to RC 146.
Cast off (bind off) loosely.

TUNIC COLLAR
Bring foward 101 (103, 107) needles on each bed to
WP. Arrange needles for full needle rib.

Using red cast on, ending with carriage at right.
Cut of red and join on navy.
MT−3, knit 32 rows. Carriage at right.
Transfer all sts to main bed. (2 sts on each needle.)
With WS of back facing, hook 47 (49, 53) sts held on
waste yarn at back neck on to centre 47 (49, 53) needles
of collar, placing sts over top of collar sts. With WS of

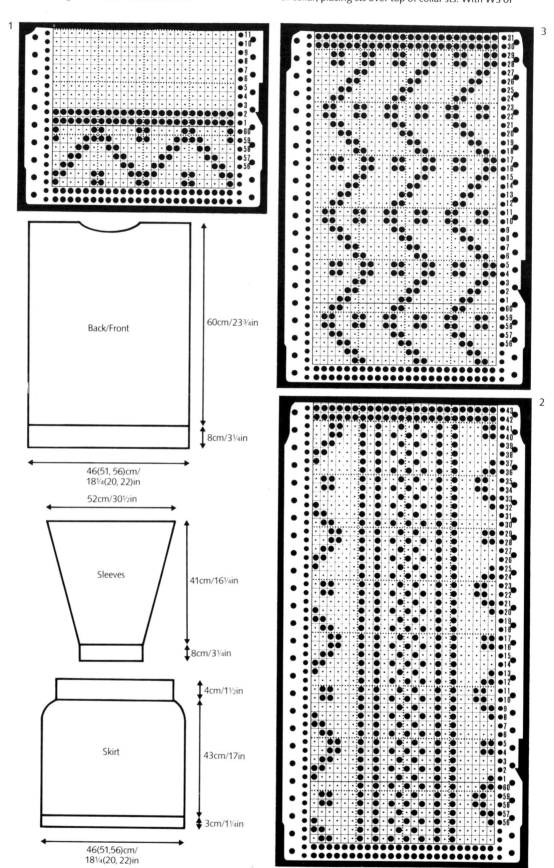

Left: The front and sleeves of Sarah Dallas' Dot'n'Zigzag tunic are patterned all over in a green dot and zigzag design.

Left: Reverse the red and green to give a brighter, bolder look.

front facing, pick up 27 sts beginning at centre front of neck to left shoulder and place on to first 27 needles of collar at right-hand side of needlebed. Using navy and casting off all sets of sts, on each needle, together, cast off (bind off) 60 sts. Gently stretching the front across the needle bed, pick up 27 sts from right side of neck, from the top of the shoulder to centre front neck, and place on to the last 27 needles at left-hand side of needlebed. Using navy, cast off (bind off) the remaining sts.

TO MAKE UP TUNIC
With RS of back facing, replace sts of both shoulders on to needles and remove waste yarn. Push sts back behind latches.
With WS of front facing, place sts of both shoulders on to same needles holding sts of back shoulders, leaving the sts in the hooks, then remove waste yarn.
Carefully push back each needle, so pulling sts of front shoulders through sts of back shoulders.
Using navy, cast off (bind off) each set of shoulder sts.
Fold sleeves in half lengthwise, then placing folds to shoulder seams, sew into position.
Join side and sleeve seams. Join row ends at centre front

of collar for approx 2cm/½in.

SKIRT (back and front alike)
Bring forward 133 (147, 163) needles on each bed to WP. Arrange needles for 1 × 1 rib.
Using red cast on, ending with carriag at right.
Cut off red and join on navy.
MT−4, knit 10 rows.
Transfer all sts to main bed.
Insert punchcard 1 and lock on first row of pattern.
Set patt into memory. RC 000.
MT. Knit 2 rows.
Working patt sequence as given in chart for border, knit to RC 19.
Continuing in navy only, knit to RC 156.
Arrange needles for 1 × 1 rib.
MT−4. RC 000. Knit 30 rows.
Cast off (bind off) loosely.

TO MAKE UP
Join side seams. Fold waistband in half to wrong side and slipstitch into place, leaving an opening for elastic. Insert elastic to fit, then close opening.

SPOT AND TWILL

MATERIALS
Rowan Botany 4 ply
600 (625, 675) g/22 (23, 24) oz in navy (shade 97)
80 (90, 100) g/3 (3½, 4) oz in coffee (shade 87)
175 (200, 225) g/7 (8, 9) oz in cream (shade 1)
Waist length of 2.5cm/1in elastic

MEASUREMENTS
To fit bust 81–86 (91–97, 102–107) cm/32–34 (36–38, 40–42) in
Actual size
Bust 104 (114, 126) cm/41 (45, 49½) in
Length 71cm/28 in
Sleeve seam 48cm/19in
Skirt length 80cm/31½in

TENSION
28 sts and 32 rows to 10cm/4in worked over Fair Isle with TD at approx 7
32 sts and 42 rows to 10cm/4in worked over st st with TD at approx 6

MACHINE
Any Brother standard gauge electronic or punchcard machine with ribbing attachment or equivalent
(If ribbing attachment not available see Alternative methods of ribbing in techniques – p.123)

BACK
Bring forward 146 (160, 176) needles on each bed to WP. Arrange needles for 1 × 1 rib.
Using navy cast on, ending with carriage at right.
MT–3, knit 30 rows.
Transfer all sts to main bed.
Insert punchcard 1 and lock on first row of pattern.
Set patt into memory. RC 000.
MT. Working patt sequence as given in chart, knit to RC 130.
Place a marker at each end of last row to denote armholes.
Continuing in patt, knit to RC 206.
Shape shoulders
Winding yarn round first needle in HP at beg of every row, place 12 (13, 15) needles at opposite end to carriage into HP at beg of next 8 rows.
Using waste yarn, knit 6 rows over rem 50 (56, 56) needles. Release sts from machine.
Return 48 (52, 60) needles at left into WP. Using waste yarn, knit 6 rows. Release sts from machine.
Return rem sts to WP. Using waste yarn, knit 6 rows. Release sts from machine.

FRONT
Work as given for back until RC 176. Carriage at right.
Shape neck
Note row on punchcard.
Place centre 28 needles into HP.
Push all needles at left of needlebed to HP.
Work on first side of neck as follows:
Using double transfer tool, dec 1 st at neck edge on next and every foll alt row until 48 (52, 60) sts rem.
Knit to RC 207.
Winding yarn round first needle in HP, place 15 sts at opposite end to carriage into HP on next and foll 2 alt rows.
Knit 2 rows. RC 214.
Using waste yarn, knit 6 rows across all shoulder sts. Release sts from machine.
Return 28 centre sts to WP.
Using waste yarn, knit 6 rows. Release sts from machine.
Return punchcard to row number previously noted.

Left: Spots and diagonal lines, separated by narrow stripes, cover the tunic top of this two piece outfit.

PATTERN SEQUENCE FOR BACK AND FRONT

ROWS	PATTERN SETTING	COLOUR IN FEEDER A	COLOUR IN FEEDER B	ROWS	PATTERN SETTING	COLOUR IN FEEDER A	COLOUR IN FEEDER B
Punchard 1 (joined into a circle)				32	plain	navy	
1–2	plain	navy		33–36	,,	coffee	
Release card				Release card			
3–31	Fair Isle	navy	cream	37–68	Fair Isle	navy	cream
Punchcard 2 Locked on row 1				69–72	plain	coffee	

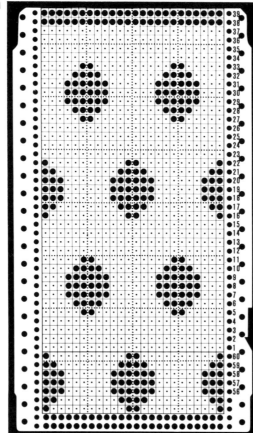

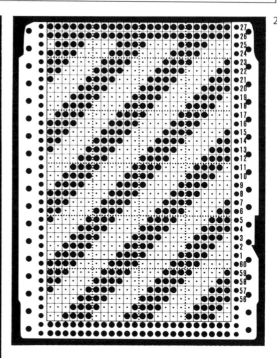

Set patt into memory. RC 176.
Return needles at left to WP.
Complete to match first side of neck, reversing all shaping.

RIGHT SLEEVE
Bring forward 76 needles on each bed to WP. Arrange needles for 1 × 1 rib.
Using navy cast on, ending with carriage at right.
MT–3, knit 30 rows.
Transfer all sts to main bed.
Insert punchcard 1 (joined into a circle) and lock on first row of pattern.
Set patt into memory. RC 000.
MT. Knit 2 rows in navy.
Set machine for Fair Isle.
With navy in feeder A and cream in feeder B, inc 1 st each end of next and every foll 3rd row until there are 114 sts. RC 57.
Then inc 1 st each end of every foll 4th row until there are 144 sts. RC 117.
Knit to RC 132.
Using navy, cast off (bind off) loosely.

LEFT SLEEVE
Work as given for right sleeve, except insert punchcard 2 instead of punchcard 1.

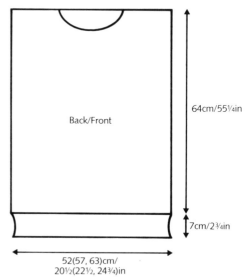

Back/Front

64cm/55¼in

7cm/2¾in

52(57, 63)cm/
20½(22½, 24¾)in

NECKBAND
Bring forward 104 (110, 110) needles on each bed to WP. Arrange needles for 1 × 1 rib.
Using navy cast on, ending with carriage at right.
MT–3, knit 11 rows. Carriage at left.
Transfer all sts to main bed.
With WS of back facing, hook 50 (56, 56) sts held on waste yarn at back neck on to first 50 (56, 56) needles of neckband, placing sts over top of neckband sts. With WS of front facing, pick up 13 sts down first side of neck and place on to next 13 needles of neckband, hook 28 sts

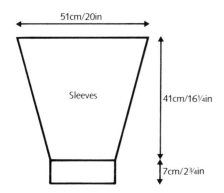

51cm/20in

Sleeves

41cm/16¼in

7cm/2¾in

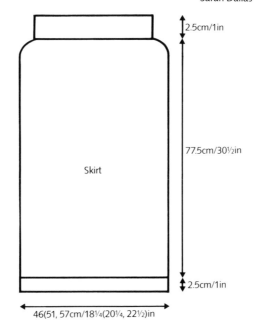

2.5cm/1in

Skirt

77.5cm/30½in

2.5cm/1in

46(51, 57cm/18¼(20¼, 22½)in

from waste yarn at centre front on to needles, then pick up 13 sts up second side of neck and hook on to needles. 104 (110, 110) sts.
MT + 1. Knit 1 row.
Cast off (bind off) loosely.

TO MAKE UP

With WS of back facing, replace sts of both shoulders on to needles and remove waste yarn. Push sts back behind latches.
With RS of front facing, place sts of both shoulders on to same needles holding sts of back shoulders, leaving the sts in the hooks, then remove waste yarn.
Carefully push back each needle, so pulling sts of front shoulders through sts of back shoulders.
Using coffee, cast off (bind off) each set of shoulder sts from right side of fabric, so forming a decorative shoulder seam.
Join neckband seam. Folds sleeves in half lengthwise, then placing folds to shoulder seams, sew into position. Join side and sleeve seams.

SKIRT (back and front alike)

Bring forward 149 (163, 183) needles on each bed to WP. Arrange needles for 1 × 1 rib.

Using navy cast on, ending with carriage at right.
MT−3, knit 10 rows.
Transfer all sts to main bed.
RC 000. MT. Working in a sequence of 26 rows navy, 4 rows cream, 26 rows navy, 4 rows coffee, knit to RC 326.
Arrange needles for 1 × 1 rib.
MT−3. RC 000. Knit 30 rows in navy.
Cast off (bind off) loosely.

TO MAKE UP

Join side seams. Fold waistband in half to wrong side and slipstitch into place, leaving an opening for elastic. Insert elastic to fit, then close opening.

Below: Broad and narrow stripes, in matching colours to the top, are worked on the skirt of this Sarah Dallas design.

SARAH DALLAS

SPOTS AND CHEVRONS

Right: The collared tunic is striped with spot and chevron bands, the spot pattern is echoed on the sleeves and there is a matching border on the otherwise plain skirt. In the background, Edy Lyngaas' Grotesque and Jane Davies' Scarp sweaters can be seen.

MATERIALS
Rowan Botany 4 ply
540 (565, 590) g/19½ (20½, 21½) oz in beige (shade 614)
70 (95, 110) g/3 (4, 4½) oz in black (shade 62)
20 (25, 30) g/1(1, 1½) oz in red (shade 45)
15 (20, 20) g/½ (1, 1) oz in gold (shade 14)
10 g/½ oz in green (shade 91)
Wasit length of 2.5 cm/1 in elastic

MEASUREMENTS
To fit bust 86 (91, 97) cm/34 (36, 38) in
Actual size
Bust 96 (102, 106) cm/38 (40, 42) in
Length 67 cm/26½ in
Sleeve seam 47 cm/18½ in
Hips 86 (92, 98) cm/34 (36, 38) in
Skirt length 50 cm/20 in

TENSION
31 sts and 39 rows to 10 cm/4 in worked over Fair Isle with TD at approx 7
33 sts and 42 rows to 10 cm/4 in worked over st st with TD at approx 6

MACHINE
Any Brother standard gauge electronic or punchcard machine with ribbing attachment or equivalent
(If ribbing attachment not available see Alternative methods of ribbing in techniques – p.123)

PATTERN SEQUENCE FOR BACK AND FRONT

ROWS	PATTERN SETTING	COLOUR IN FEEDER A	COLOUR IN FEEDER B	ROWS	PATTERN SETTING	COLOUR IN FEEDER A	COLOUR IN FEEDER B
Punchcard 1A and 1B (joined into a circle)							
				44–46	Fair Isle	beige	black
1–20	Fair Isle	beige	black	47–48	plain	beige	
21	plain	beige		49–51	Fair Isle	beige	black
22	,,	red		52–53	plain	beige	
23–24	,,	beige		54	,,	red	
25–28	Fair Isle	beige	gold	55–56	,,	beige	
29–30	plain	beige		57–60	Fair Isle	beige	green
31	,,	red		61–62	plain	beige	
32–33	,,	beige		63	,,	red	
34–36	Fair Isle	beige	black	64	,,	beige	
37–38	plain	beige					
39–41	Fair Isle	beige	black	Rep rows 1 to 64 throughout.			
42–43	plain	beige					

TUNIC BACK
Bring forward 158 (168, 174) needles on each bed to WP. Arrange needles for 1 × 1 rib.
Using black cast on, ending with carriage at right.
Cut off black and join on beige.
MT−3, knit 14 rows.
Transfer all sts to main bed.
Insert punchcard and lock on first row of pattern.
Set patt into memory. RC 000.
MT. Knit 2 rows in beige.
Working patt sequence as given in chart, knit to RC 156.
Place a marker at each end of last row to denote beginning of armholes.
Continuing in patt, knit to RC 225.
Remove punchcard 1 and insert punchcard 2, knit 2 rows beige, then with beige in feeder A and black in feeder B, knit to RC 248.
Shape shoulders
Winding yarn round first needle in HP at beg of every row, place 14 (15, 15) needles at opposite end to carriage into HP at beg of next 8 rows. Using waste yarn, knit 6 rows over rem 46 (48, 54) needles, Release sts from machine. Return 56 (60, 60) needles at left into WP. Using waste yarn, knit 6 rows. Release sts from machine. Return rem sts to WP. Using waste yarn, knit 6 rows. Release sts from machine.

TUNIC FRONT
Work as given for back until RC 236. Carriage at right.
Shape neck
Note row on punchcard.
Place centre 22 (24, 30) needles into HP.
Push all needles at left of needlebed to HP.
Work on first side of neck as follows:
Dec 1 st at neck edge on next 12 rows.
Knit 1 row. RC 249.
Winding yarn round first needle in HP, place 14 (15, 15) needles at opposite end to carriage into HP on next and foll 2 alt rows.
Knit 2 rows. RC 255.
Using waste yarn, knit 6 rows. Release sts from machine.
Return 22 (24, 30) centre needles to WP.
Using waste yarn, knit 6 rows. Release sts from machine.
Return punchcard to row number previously noted.
Sett patt into memory. RC 236.
Return needles at left to WP.
Complete to match first side of neck, reversing all shaping.

TUNIC SLEEVES
Bring forward 82 needles on each bed to WP. Arrange needles for 1 × 1 rib.
Using black cast on, ending with carriage at right.
Cut off black and join on beige.

PATTERN SEQUENCE FOR SLEEVES

ROWS	PATTERN SETTING	COLOUR IN FEEDER A	COLOUR IN FEEDER B
Punchcard 2 (joined into a circle)			
1–3	Fair Isle	beige	black
4–5	plain	beige	
Rep rows 1 to 5 throughout.			

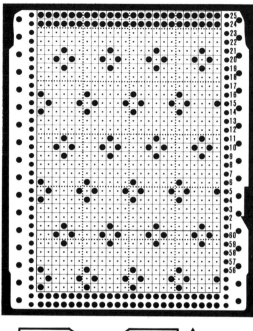

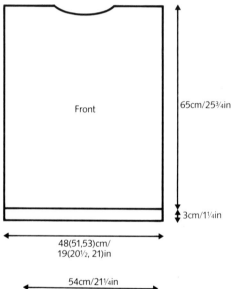

1B

1A

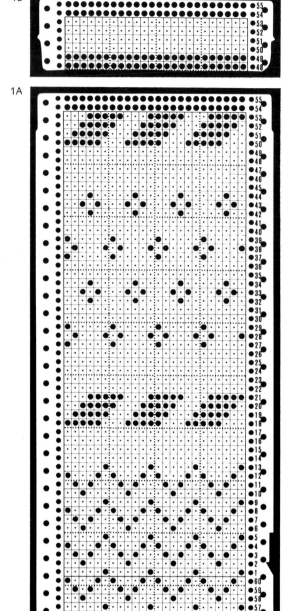

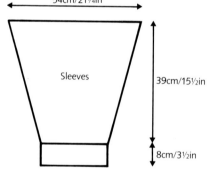

Front

65cm/25¾in

3cm/1¼in

48(51,53)cm/
19(20½, 21)in

54cm/21¼in

Sleeves

39cm/15½in

8cm/3½in

MT−3, knit 32 rows.
Transfer all sts to main bed.
Insert punchcard 2 and lock on first row of pattern.
Sett patt into memory. RC 000.
MT. Knit 2 rows in beige.
Working pat sequence as given in chart for sleeves, inc 1 st each end of every 3rd row until there are 114 sts. RC 50.
Inc 1 st each end of every foll 4th row until there are 166 sts. RC 154.
Using beige, cast off (bind off) loosely.

TUNIC COLLAR
Bring forward 100 (102, 108) needles on each bed to WP. Arrange needles for 1 × 1 rib.
Using black cast on, ending with carriage at right.
Cut off black and join on beige.
MT−3, knit 40 rows. Carriage at right.
Transfer all sts to main bed.
With WS of back facing, hook 46 (48, 54) sts held on waste yarn at back neck on to centre 46 (48, 54) needles of collar, placing sts over top of collar sts. With WS of

front facing, piack up 27 sts from centre front of neck to left shoulder and place on to first 27 needles of collar.
Using beige and casting off both sets of sts together, cast off (bind off) 60 sts. Gently stretching the front across the needle bed, pick up 27 sts from right side of neck, from the top of the shoulder to centre front neck, and place on to the last 27 needles. Using beige, cast off (bind off) the remaining sts.

TO MAKE UP TUNIC
With RS of back facing, replace sts of both shoulders on to needles and remove waste yarn. Push sts back behind latches.

Left: Different effects can be achieved with this pattern, depending on whether the background is dark or light.

With WS of front facing, place sts of both shoulders on to same needles holding sts of back shoulders, leaving the sts in the hooks, then remove waste yarn.
Carefully push back each needle, so pulling sts of front shoulders through sts of back shoulders. Using beige, cast off (bind off) each set of shoulder sts.
Unravel all waste yarn. Folds sleeves in half lengthwise, then placing folds to shoulder seams, sew into position.
Join side and sleeve seams.

SKIRT (back and front alike)
Bring forward 133 (143, 149) needles on each bed to WP. Arrange needles for 1 × 1 rib.
Using black cast on, ending with carriage at right.
Cut off black and join on beige.
MT−3, knit 10 rows.
Transfer all sts to main bed.
Insert punchcard 1 and lock on row 21 of pattern.
Set patt into memory. RC 000.
Knit 2 rows in beige. MT for Fair Isle.
Work rows 21 to 31 of patt sequence as given in chart for back and front of tunic.
Set MT for st st.
Continuing in beige only, knit to RC 204. Arrange needles for 1 × 1 rib.

Skirt

4cm/1½in

48cm/19in

2cm/¾in

43(46,48)cm/
17(18¼, 19)in

MT−3. RC 000. Knit 30 rows.
Cast off (bind off) loosely.

TO MAKE UP
Join side seams. Fold waistband in half to wrong side and slipstitch into place, leaving an opening for elastic. Insert elastic to fit, then close opening.

JANE DAVIES

ROSIE

Right: The small roses are worked all in one colour, but the larger ones are formed by using three toning shades.

MATERIALS

Rowan Cabled Mercerised Cotton 4 ply
350 (400) g/13 (14) oz in cream (shade 301)
50g/2oz in red (shade 321)
50g/2oz in pastel peach (shade 313)
50g/2oz in apricot (shade 304)
Rowan Sea Breeze 4 ply
150 (200) g/6 (7) oz in mermaid (shade 547)
50g/2oz in antique pink (shade 533)
50g/2oz in rain cloud (shade 528)
Rowan Salad Days 4 ply
50g/2oz in viola (shade 573)
50g/2oz in bright pink (shade 568)
50g/2oz in hyacinth (shade 566)
50g/2oz in electric blue (shade 570)
50g/2oz in sunshine (shade 567)

MEASUREMENTS

To fit bust 86–91 (97–107) cm/34–36 (38–42) in
Actual size
Bust 106 (120) cm/42 (47½) in
Length 67cm/26½in
Sleeve seam 46cm/18¼in

TENSION

30 sts and 33 rows to 10cm/4in worked over st st with TD at approx 8

MACHINE

Any Brother standard gauge electronic or punchcard machine with ribbing attachment or equivalent
(If ribbing attachment not available see Alternative methods of ribbing in techniques – p.123)

PATTERN SEQUENCE FOR BACK AND FRONT

ROWS	PATTERN SETTING	COLOUR IN FEEDER A	COLOUR IN FEEDER B	ROWS	PATTERN SETTING	COLOUR IN FEEDER A	COLOUR IN FEEDER B
Punchcard 1 (joined into a circle)				104–106	,,	cream	rain cloud
1–4	Fair Isle	cream	mermaid	107–108	plain	cream	
5–9	,,	cream	antique pink	109–114	Fair Isle	cream	mermaid
10–13	plain	cream		115–116	,,	cream	sunshine
14–17	Fair Isle	cream	mermaid	117–118	,,	cream	apricot
18–22	,,	cream	rain cloud	119–121	,,	cream	pastel peach
23–26	plain	cream		122–123	plain	cream	
27–30	Fair Isle	cream	mermaid	124–129	Fair Isle	cream	mermaid
31–35	,,	cream	viola	130–131	,,	cream	hyacinth
36–39	plain	cream		132–133	,,	cream	antique pink
40–43	Fair Isle	cream	mermaid	134–136	,,	cream	pastel peach
44–48	,,	cream	bright pink	137–138	plain	cream	
49–52	plain	cream		139–144	Fair Isle	cream	mermaid
53–56	Fair Isle	cream	mermaid	145–146	,,	cream	rain cloud
57–61	,,	cream	red	147–148	,,	cream	hyacinth
62-65	plain	cream		149–151	,,	cream	viola
66–69	Fair Isle	cream	mermaid	152–153	plain	cream	
70–74	,,	cream	hyacinth	154–159	Fair Isle	cream	mermaid
Insert punchcard 2 (joined into a circle)				160–161	,,	cream	antique pink
Lock on row 1				162–163	,,	cream	red
75–78	plain	cream		164–166	,,	cream	bright pink
Release card				167–168	plain	cream	
79–84	Fair Isle	cream	mermaid	169–174	Fair Isle	cream	mermaid
85–86	,,	cream	pastel peach	175–176	,,	cream	hyacinth
87–88	,,	cream	antique pink	177–178	,,	cream	viola
89–91	,,	cream	red	179–181	,,	cream	electric blue
92–93	plain	cream		182–183	plain	cream	
94–99	Fair Isle	cream	mermaid	184–189	Fair Isle	cream	mermaid
100–101	,,	cream	electric blue	190–191	,,	cream	antique pink
102–103	,,	cream	viola	192–193	,,	cream	red
				194–196	,,	cream	sunshine
				197–200	plain	cream	

BACK

Bring forward 149 (169) needles on each bed to WP.
Arrange needles for 1 × 1 rib.
Using cream cast on, ending with carriage at right.
MT–3, knit 31 rows.
Work 6 rows waste yarn and release work from machine.
Bring forward 160 (180) needles on main bed to WP. Carriage at left.
With WS of work facing, hook sts from last row worked in cream evenly over the needles, increasing sts as necessary along the bed.

Insert punchcard and lock on first row of pattern.
Set patt into memory.
Using cream, knit 1 row. RC 000. MT.
Working patt sequence as given in chart, knit to RC 122.
Shape armholes
Keeping patt sequence correct, dec 1 st each end of next 10 rows. RC 132.
140 (160) sts. Knit to RC 200.
Place centre 50 needles into HP. Place needles at left into HP.
Using waste yarn, knit 6 rows over rem needles.
Release sts from machine.

PATTERN SEQUENCE FOR SLEEVES

ROWS	PATTERN SETTING	COLOUR IN FEEDER A	COLOUR IN FEEDER B	ROWS	PATTERN SETTING	COLOUR IN FEEDER A	COLOUR IN FEEDER B
Work as given for back and front to RC 74.				Lock on row 1			
75–78	plain	cream		114–117	plain	cream	
79–82	Fair Isle	cream	mermaid	Release card			
83–87	,,	cream	pastel peach	118–123	Fair Isle	cream	mermaid
88–91	plain	cream		124–125	,,	cream	hyacinth
92–95	Fair Isle	cream	mermaid	126–127	,,	cream	antique pink
96–100	,,	cream	electric blue	128–130	,,	cream	pastel peach
101–104	plain	cream		131–134	plain	cream	
105–108	Fair Isle	cream	mermaid				
109–113	,,	cream	antique pink				
Insert punchcard 2 (joined into a circle)							

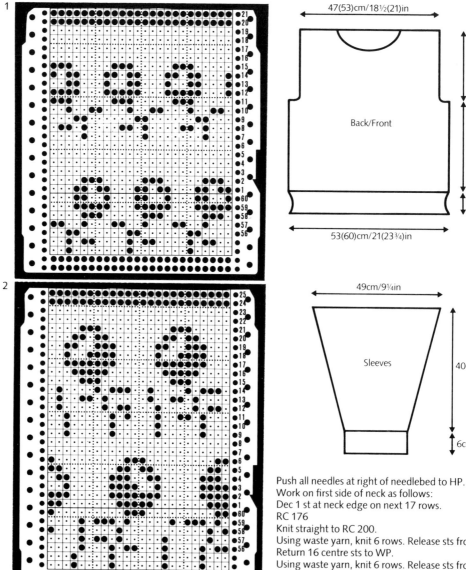

Return 45 (55) needles at left into WP. Using waste yarn, knit 6 rows. Release sts from machine.
Return rem sts to WP. Using waste yarn, knit 6 rows. Release sts from machine.

FRONT

Work as given for back until RC 159. Carriage at left.
Note row on punchcard.
Shape neck
Place centre 16 needles into HP.

Push all needles at right of needlebed to HP.
Work on first side of neck as follows:
Dec 1 st at neck edge on next 17 rows.
RC 176
Knit straight to RC 200.
Using waste yarn, knit 6 rows. Release sts from machine.
Return 16 centre sts to WP.
Using waste yarn, knit 6 rows. Release sts from machine.
Return punchcard to row number previously noted.
Set patt into memory. RC 159.
Return needles at right to WP.
Complete to match first side of neck, reversing all shaping.

SLEEVES

Bring forward 61 needles on each bed to WP. Arrange needles for 1 × 1 rib.
Using cream cast on, ending with carriage at right.
MT–3, knit 31 rows.
Work 6 rows waste yarn and release work from machine.

Left: Work each row of flowers in a different colour if you wish; an ideal way of using up all those oddments.

Bring forward 84 needles on main bed to WP.
Carriage at left.
With WS of work facing, hook sts from last row worked in cream evenly over the needles, increasing sts as necessary along the bed.
Insert punchcard and lock on first row of pattern.
Set patt into memory.
MT. Using cream, knit 1 row.
Working patt sequence as given in chart for sleeves, inc 1 st each end of every 6th row until there are 148 sts.
Knit straight to RC 134.
Cast off (bind off) loosely).

NECKBAND
Bring forward 136 needles on main bed to WP.
Arrange needles for 1 × 1 rib.
With WS of back facing, hook 50 sts held on waste yarn at back neck on to first 50 needles of neckband, placing sts over top of neckband sts.
With WS of front facing, pick up 35 sts down first side of neck and place on to next 35 needles of neckband, hook 16 sts from waste yarn at centre front on to needles, then pick up 35 sts up second side of neck and hook on to needles. 136 sts.
Insert punchcard 1 and lock on row 5.

With cream, knit 2 rows.
Set machine for Fair Isle.
Release card
With cream in feeder A and pastel peach in feeder B, knit 5 rows.
Set machine for plain knitting and knit 2 rows.
Arrange needles for 1 × 1 rib.
MT-3. Knit 17 rows.
Cast off (bind off) loosely.

TO MAKE UP
With RS of back facing, replace sts of both shoulders on to needles and remove waste yarn. Push sts back behind latches.
With WS of front facing, place sts of both shoulders on to same needles holding sts of back shoulders, leaving the sts in the hooks, then remove waste yarn.
Carefully push back each needle, so pulling sts of front shoulders through sts of back shoulders.
Using cream, cast off (bind off) each set of shoulder sts.
Join neckband seam. Fold neckband in half to WS and slipstitch down.
Folds sleeves in half lengthwise, then placing folds to shoulder seams, sew into position. Join side and sleeve seams.

JANE DAVIES

NAVAHO

Right: The woman's version shown here is knitted with pale blue cuffs and welts as given in the pattern, as an alternative, try knitting in rich autumn shades as seen on the man's version.

MATERIALS

Rowan Lightweight Double Knitting
205 (230, 255) g/8 (9, 9½) oz in pale blue (shade 48)
100 (125, 150) g/4 (5, 6) oz in salmon (shade 103)
135 (160, 185) g/5½ (6½, 7½) oz in mid blue (shade 52)
25 (30, 35) g/1 (1½, 2) oz in brick (shade 23)
65 (70, 75) g/2 (2½, 3) oz in beige (shade 615)

MEASUREMENTS

To fit chest/bust 81–86 (91-97, 102–107) cm/32–34 (36–38, 40–42) in
Actual size
Chest/bust 96 (106, 116) cm/38 (42, 46) in

Length 67cm/26½in
Sleeve seam 47cm/18½in

TENSION

31 sts and 33 rows to 10cm/4in worked over Fair Isle with TD at approx 8

MACHINE

Any Brother standard gauge electronic or punchcard machine with ribbing attachment or equivalent
(If ribbing attachment not available see Alternative methods of ribbing in techniques – p.123)

PATTERN SEQUENCE FOR BACK AND FRONT

ROWS	PATTERN SETTING	COLOUR IN FEEDER A	COLOUR IN FEEDER B	ROWS	PATTERN SETTING	COLOUR IN FEEDER A	COLOUR IN FEEDER B
Punchcard 1				Punchcards 3a and b (joined together)			
1–13	Fair Isle	salmon	mid blue	65–72	Fair Isle	pale blue	salmon
14	,,	salmon	brick	73–88	,,	mid blue	salmon
15	,,	beige	brick	89–94	,,	brick	salmon ·
16–24	,,	beige	mid blue	95–98	,,	brick	mid blue
25	plain	salmon		99–112	,,	beige	mid blue
Punchcard 2 (joined into circle)				113–128	,,	salmon	mid blue
				129-132	,,	salmon	brick
26–38	Fair Isle	pale blue	beige	133–142	,,	pale blue	brick
39–51	,,	pale blue	salmon	Punchcard 2 (insert upside down then join into circle)			
52–64	,,	pale blue	mid blue	143–155	Fair Isle	pale blue	beige
				156–168	,,	pale blue	mid blue
				169–181	,,	pale blue	salmon
				182–194	,,	pale blue	mid blue
				195–196	plain	pale blue	

PATTERN SEQUENCE FOR SLEEVES

ROWS	PATTERN SETTING	COLOUR IN FEEDER A	COLOUR IN FEEDER B	ROWS	PATTERN SETTING	COLOUR IN FEEDER A	COLOUR IN FEEDER B
Punchcard 1				Release card			
1-13	Fair Isle	salmon	mid blue	61–72	Fair Isle	pale blue	beige
14	,,	salmon	brick	Lock card			
15	,,	beige	brick	73–84	plain	salmon	
16–24	,,	beige	mid blue	Release card			
Punchcard 3a and 3b (joined together)				85–96	Fair Isle	beige	mid blue
Lock card on row 19				Lock card			
25–36	plain	pale blue		97–108	plain	brick	
Release card				Release card			
37–48	Fair Isle	salmon	brick	109–132	Fair Isle	mid blue	salmon
Lock card							
49–60	plain	mid blue					

BACK

Bring forward 137 (153, 169) needles on each bed to WP. Arrange needles for 1 × 1 rib.
Using pale blue cast on, ending with carriage at right.
MT–3, knit 30 rows.
Work 6 rows waste yarn and release work from machine.
Bring forward 148 (164, 180) needles on main bed to WP. Carriage at right.
With WS of work facing, hook sts from last row worked in pale blue evenly over the needles, increasing sts as necessary along the bed.
Insert punchcard and lock on first row of pattern.
MT-1. Using pale blue, knit 2 rows.
Set patt into memory. RC 000.
MT. Working patt sequence as given in chart,

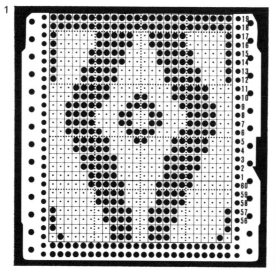

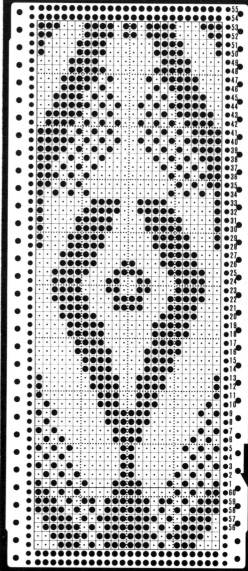

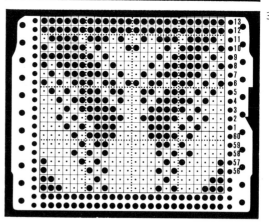

knit to RC 118.
Shape armholes.
Keeping patt sequence correct, dec 1 st each end of next 10 rows. RC 128
128 (144, 160) sts. Knit to RC 196.
Place centre 50 needles into HP. Place needles at left into HP.
Using waste yarn, knit 6 rows over rem needles.
Release sts from machine.
Return 39 (47, 55) needles at left into WP. Using waste yarn, knit 6 rows. Release sts from machine.
Return rem sts to WP. Using waste yarn, knit 6 rows. Release sts from machine.

FRONT
Work as given for back until RC 154. Carriage at right.
Shape neck
Note row on punchcard.
Place centre 10 needles into HP.
Push all needles at left of needlebed to HP.
Work on first side of neck as follows:
Dec 1 st at neck edge on next 20 rows.
RC 174
Knit straight to RC 196.
Using waste yarn, knit 6 rows. Release sts from machine.
Return 10 centre sts to WP.
Using waste yarn, knit 6 rows. Release sts from machine.
Return punchcard to row number previously noted.
Set patt into memory. RC 154.
Return needles at left to WP.
Complete to match first side of neck, reversing all shaping.

SLEEVES
Bring forward 61 needles on each bed to WP. Arrange needles for 1 × 1 rib.
Using pale blue cast on, ending with carriage at right.
MT−3, knit 30 rows.
Work 6 rows waste yarn and release work from machine.
Bring forward 84 needles on main bed to WP.
Carriage at right.
With WS of work facing, hook sts from last row worked in pale blue evenly over the needles, increasing sts as necessary along the bed.

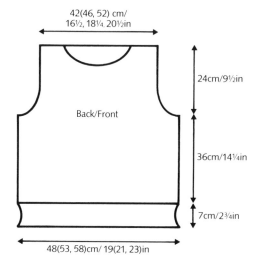

42(46, 52) cm/
16½, 18¼, 20½in

Back/Front

24cm/9½in

36cm/14¼in

7cm/2¾in

48(53, 58)cm/ 19(21, 23)in

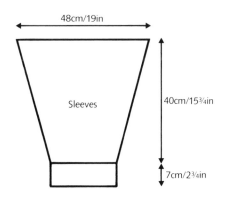

48cm/19in

Sleeves

40cm/15¾in

7cm/2¾in

*Above: A fairly simple
pattern repeat forms the
design on Jane Davies'
Navaho sweaters. The
pattern on the sleeves is
broken with plain bands of
colour.*

Insert punchcard and lock on first row of pattern.
MT−1. Using pale blue, knit 2 rows.
Set patt into memory. RC 000.
MT. Working patt sequence as given in chart for sleeves,
inc 1 st each end of every 4th row until there are 148 sts.
Knit straight to RC 132.
Set machine for plain knitting.
Knit 1 row in mid blue.
Cast off (bind off) loosely.

NECKBAND
Bring forward 135 needles on each bed to WP.
Arrange needles for 1 × 1 rib.
Using pale blue cast on, ending with carriage at right.
MT−3, knit 21 rows. Carriage at left.
Transfer all sts to main bed.
With WS of back facing, hook 50 sts held on waste yarn
at back neck on to first 50 needles of neckband, placing
sts over top of neckband sts.

With WS of front facing, pick up 38 ss down first side of
neck and place on to next 38 needles of neckband, hook
10 sts from waste yarn at centre front on to needles,
then pick up 38 sts up second side of neck and hook on
to needles. 136 sts.
MT + 1. Knit 1 row.
Cast off (bind off) loosely.

TO MAKE UP
With RS of back facing, replace sts of both shoulders on
to needles and remove waste yarn. Push sts back behind
latches.
With WS of front facing, place sts of both shoulders on
to same needles holding sts of back shoulders, leaving
the sts in the hooks, then remove waste yarn.
Carefully push back each needle, so pulling sts of front
shoulders through sts of back shoulders.
Using pale blue, cast off (bind off) each set of shoulder
sts.
Unravel all waste yarn. Join shoulder and neckband
seams. Fold neckband in half to WS and slipstitch down.
Fold sleeves in half lengthwise, then placing folds to
shoulder seams, sew into position. Join side and sleeve
seams.

JANE DAVIES

SCARP SWEATER

Right: In warm, bright colours this sweater is easier to knit than it looks.

MATERIALS
Rowan Fine Fleck Tweed
200 (225) g/8 (9) oz in black (shade 62)
150 (175) g/6 (7) oz in red (shade 44)
Rowan Light Tweed
100 (125) g/4 (5) oz in cherrymix (shade 261)
Rowan Botany 4 ply
100 (125) g/4 (5) oz in brown (shade 602)
100 (125) g/4 (5) oz in brick (shade 26)

MEASUREMENTS
To fit chest/bust 91–102 (107–112) cm/36–40 (42–44) in
Actual size

Chest/bust 114 (126) cm/45 (49½) in
Length 64cm/25¼in
Sleeve seam 50cm/19¾in

TENSION
30 sts and 36 rows to 10cm/4in worked over st st with TD at approx 8

MACHINE
Any Brother standard gauge electronic or punchcard machine with ribbing attachment or equivalent (If ribbing attachment not available see Alternative methods of ribbing in techniques – p.123)

PATTERN SEQUENCE FOR BACK, FRONT AND SLEEVES

ROWS	PATTERN SETTING	COLOUR IN FEEDER A	COLOUR IN FEEDER B
Punchcard 1 (for border)			
Release card			
1–2	Fair Isle	black	cherrymix
3–5	,,	brown	cherrymix
6–7	plain	brown	
8–16	Fair Isle	brown	red
17–19	,,	brick	red
20–28	,,	brown	brick
29–30	plain	brown	
31–33	Fair Isle	brown	cherrymix
34–35	,,	black	cherrymix

Insert punchcard 2 (joined into a circle)
Keeping A in feeder A throughout, work 2 rows plain and 13 rows Fair Isle, following the sequence of 2 rows E, 2 rows B, 2 rows D when working Fair Isle to RC 125.
Insert punchard 3
Lock on row 1

ROWS	PATTERN SETTING	COLOUR IN FEEDER A	COLOUR IN FEEDER B
126–27	plain	black	
Release card			
128–129	Fair Isle	black	red
130–136	,,	brown	red

ROWS	PATTERN SETTING	COLOUR IN FEEDER A	COLOUR IN FEEDER B
137–139	,,	brick	red
140–146	,,	brown	red
147–148	,,	black	red

Insert punchcard 2 (joined into a circle)
Keeping A in feeder A throughout, work 2 rows plain and 13 rows Fair Isle, following the sequence of 2 rows E, 2 rows B, 2 rows D when working Fair Isle to RC 193.
Insert punchcard 4 (joined into a circle)
Lock on row 1

ROWS	PATTERN SETTING	COLOUR IN FEEDER A	COLOUR IN FEEDER B
194	plain	black	
Release card			
195–198	tuck	cherrymix	
199–200	plain	black	
201–204	tuck	brick	
205–206	plain	black	
207–210	tuck	cherrymix	
211–212	plain	black	
213–216	tuck	red	
217–218	plain	black	
219–222	tuck	brown	
223–224	plain	black	

BACK
Bring forward 160 (180) needles on each bed to WP.
Arrange needles for 2 × 2 rib.
Using black cast on, ending with carriage at right.
MT−3, knit 36 rows.
Work 6 rows waste yarn and release work from machine.
Bring forward 170 (190) needles on main bed to WP.
Carriage at right.
With WS of work facing, hook sts from last row worked in black evenly over the needles, increasing sts as necessary along the bed.
Insert punchcard and lock on first row of pattern.
Set patt into memory. RC 000.
MT. Working patt sequence as given in chart, knit to RC 224.
Place centre 50 needles into HP. Place needles at left into HP.
Using waste yarn, knit 6 rows over rem needles.
Release sts from machine.
Return 60 (70) needles at left into WP. Using waste yarn, knit 6 rows. Release sts from machine.
Return rem sts to WP. Using waste yarn, knit 6 rows. Release sts from machine.

FRONT
Work as given for back until RC 178.
Carriage at right.
Note row on punchcard.
Shape neck
Place centre 16 needles into HP.
Push all needles at left of needlebed to HP.
Work on first side of neck as follows:
Dec 1 st at neck edge on next 17 rows. RC 195
Knit straight to RC 224.
Using waste yarn, knit 6 rows. Release sts from machine.
Return 16 centre sts to WP.
Using waste yarn, knit 6 rows. Release sts from machine.
Return punchcard to row number previously noted.
Set patt into memory. RC 178.
Return needles at left to WP.
Complete to match first side of neck, reversing all shaping.

SLEEVES
Bring forward 62 needles on each bed to WP. Arrange needles for 2 × 2 rib.
Using black cast on, ending with carriage at right.

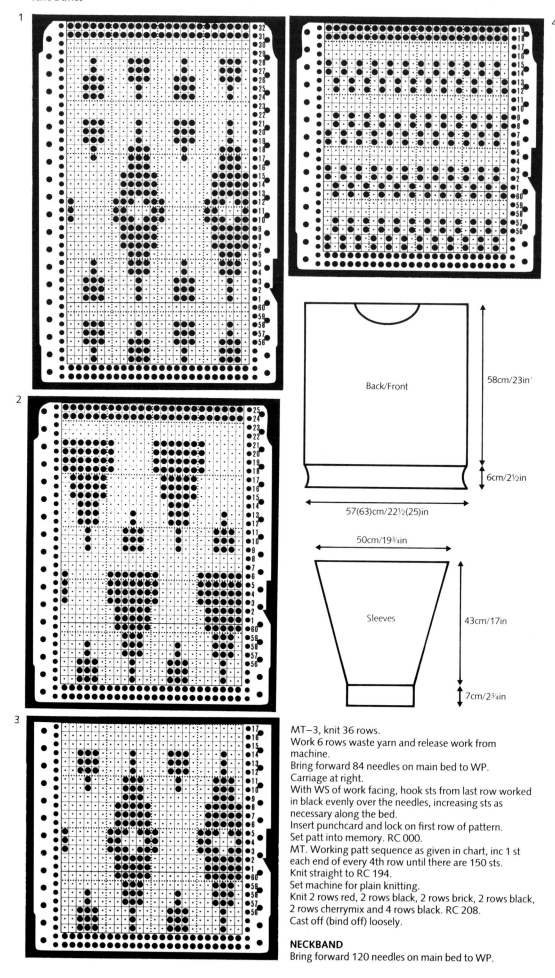

MT−3, knit 36 rows.
Work 6 rows waste yarn and release work from machine.
Bring forward 84 needles on main bed to WP.
Carriage at right.
With WS of work facing, hook sts from last row worked in black evenly over the needles, increasing sts as necessary along the bed.
Insert punchcard and lock on first row of pattern.
Set patt into memory. RC 000.
MT. Working patt sequence as given in chart, inc 1 st each end of every 4th row until there are 150 sts.
Knit straight to RC 194.
Set machine for plain knitting.
Knit 2 rows red, 2 rows black, 2 rows brick, 2 rows black, 2 rows cherrymix and 4 rows black. RC 208.
Cast off (bind off) loosely.

NECKBAND
Bring forward 120 needles on main bed to WP.

Left: The man's version of the Scarp Sweater is knitted in soft, muted brown and beige tweeds with a splash of black to add interest.

With WS of back facing, hook 50 sts from centre back neck on to first 50 needles. With WS of front facing, pick up 27 sts down first side of neck and place on to next 27 needles, hook 16 sts from centre front neck on to next 16 needles, then pick up 27 sts up second side of neck and place on to last 27 needles.
Insert punchcard 4 and lock on first row of patt.
Knit 2 rows black.
Release card.
Tuck 2 rows red, knit 2 rows black, tuck 2 rows brick, knit 2 rows black, tuck 2 rows cherrymix, then using black only knit to RC 30.
Make hem by picking up loops from first row and placing on to needles.
MT + 1. Knit 1 row black.

Cast off (bind off) loosely.

TO MAKE UP
With RS of back facing, replace sts of both shoulders on to needles and remove waste yarn. Push sts back behind latches.
With WS of front facing, place sts of both shoulders on to same needles holding sts of back shoulders, leaving the sts in the hooks, then remove waste yarn.
Carefully push back each needle, so pulling sts of front shoulders through sts of back shoulders.
Using black, cast off (bind off) each set of shoulder sts.
Join seam. Folds sleeves in half lengthwise, then placing folds to shoulder seams, sew into position.
Join side and sleeve seams.

JANE DAVIES
WAISTCOAT

Right: The rich colours of this diagonal patterned waistcoat adds interest to the plainest outfit. A good example of Jane Davies' ability to mix unusual colours together.

MATERIALS
Rowan Cabled Mercerised Cotton
200g/8oz in rich purple (shade 310)
50g/2oz in claret (shade 315)
50g/2oz in black (shade 319)
50g/2oz in deep blue (shade 309)
Rowan Fine Cotton Chenille
50g/2oz in purple (shade 384)
50g/2oz in cardinal (shade 379)
50g/2oz in lacquer (shade 388)
50g/2oz in cyclamen (shade 385)
Rowan Salad Days
50g/2oz in cornflower (shade 573)
50g/2oz in electric blue (shade 570)
Rowan Sea Breeze
50g/2oz in frolic (shade 534)
50g/2oz in rain cloud (shade 528)
50g/2oz in signal red (shade 532)

MEASUREMENTS
To fit bust 86–97cm/34–38in
Actual size
Bust 102cm/40¼in
Length 56cm/22in

TENSION
27 sts and 36 rows to 10cm/4in worked over st st with TD at approx 9

MACHINE
Any Brother standard gauge electronic or punchcard machine or equivalent

PATTERN SEQUENCE FOR BACK AND FRONT BORDERS

ROWS	PATTERN SETTING	COLOUR IN FEEDER A	COLOUR IN FEEDER B
Punchcard 1 (joined into a circle)			
Release card			
1–2	Fair Isle	rich purple	purple chenille
3	plain	rich purple	
4–9	Fair Isle	rich purple	bright blue
10	plain	rich purple	
11	Fair Isle	rich purple	frolic
12	,,	claret	frolic
13	plain	claret	
14–19	Fair Isle	claret	black
20	plain	claret	
21	Fair Isle	claret	rain cloud
22	,,	deep blue	rain cloud
23	plain	deep blue	
24–29	Fair Isle	deep blue	cardinal
30	plain	deep blue	
31	Fair Isle	deep blue	signal red
32	,,	black	signal red
33	plain	black	
34–39	Fair Isle	black	cyclamen
40	plain	black	
Insert punchcard 2 (joined into a circle)			
Set patt into memory			
41	Fair Isle	black	rich purple
42	Fair Isle	claret	rich purple
43–44	plain	claret	
45–50	Fair Isle	claret	rich purple
51–52	plain	claret	
53	Fair Isle	claret	signal red
54	,,	bright blue	signal red
55–56	plain	bright blue	
57–62	Fair Isle	bright blue	black
63–64	plain	bright blue	
65	Fair Isle	bright blue	lacquer
66	,,	cornflower	lacquer
67–68	plain	cornflower	
69–74	Fair Isle	cornflower	frolic
75–76	plain	cornflower	
77	Fair Isle	cornflower	cardinal
78	,,	rich purple	cardinal
79–80	plain	rich purple	
81–86	Fair Isle	rich purple	rain cloud
87–88	plain	rich purple	
89	Fair Isle	rich purple	black
90	,,	cardinal	black
91–92	plain	cardinal	
93–98	Fair Isle	cardinal	deep blue
99–100	plain	cardinal	
101	Fair Isle	cardinal	signal red
102	,,	black	signal red
103–104	plain	black	
105–110	Fair Isle	black	purple chenille
111–112	plain	black	
113	Fair Isle	black	rain cloud
114	,,	claret	rain cloud
115–116	plain	claret	
117–122	Fair Isle	claret	rich purple
123–124	plain	claret	
125	Fair Isle	claret	cornflower
126	,,	deep blue	cornflower
127–128	plain	deep blue	
129–134	Fair Isle	deep blue	signal red
135–136	plain	deep blue	
137	Fair Isle	deep blue	frolic
138	,,	cardinal	frolic
139–140	plain	cardinal	
141–146	Fair Isle	cardinal	bright blue
147–148	plain	cardinal	
149	Fair Isle	cardinal	black
150	,,	purple chenille	black
151–152	plain	purple chenille	
153–158	Fair Isle	purple chenille	rich purple
159–160	plain	purple chenille	
161	Fair Isle	purple chenille	signal red
162	,,	lacquer	signal red
163–164	plain	lacquer	
165–170	Fair Isle	lacquer	frolic
171–172	plain	lacquer	
173	Fair Isle	lacquer	bright blue
174	,,	cornflower	bright blue
175–176	plain	cornflower	
177–182	Fair Isle	cornflower	rain cloud
183–184	plain	cornflower	
185	Fair Isle	cornflower	frolic
186	,,	black	frolic
187–188	plain	black	
189–194	Fair Isle	black	cardinal
195–196	plain	black	
197	Fair Isle	black	signal red
198	,,	rich purple	signal red

PATTERN SEQUENCE FOR FRONT (MAIN PART)

ROWS	PATTERN SETTING	COLOUR IN FEEDER A	COLOUR IN FEEDER B	ROWS	PATTERN SETTING	COLOUR IN FEEDER A	COLOUR IN FEEDER B
Punchcard 1 (joined into a circle)				80	,,	cardinal	frolic
				81	plain	cardinal	
Release card				82–87	Fair Isle	cardinal	bright blue
				88	plain	cardinal	
1	plain	claret		89	Fair Isle	cardinal	black
2–7	Fair Isle	claret	rich purple	90	,,	purple chenille	black
8	plain	claret		91	plain	purple chenille	
9	Fair Isle	claret	signal red	92–97	Fair Isle	purple chenille	rich purple
10	,,	bright blue	signal red	98	plain	purple chenille	
11	plain	bright blue		99	Fair Isle	purple chenille	signal red
12–17	Fair Isle	bright blue	black	100	,,	lacquer	signal red
18	plain	bright blue		101	plain	lacquer	
19	Fair Isle	bright blue	lacquer	102–107	Fair Isle	lacquer	frolic
20	,,	cornflower	lacquer	108	plain	lacquer	
21	plain	cornflower		109	Fair Isle	lacquer	bright blue
22–27	Fair Isle	cornflower	frolic	110	,,	cornflower	bright blue
28	plain	cornflower		111	plain	cornflower	
29	Fair Isle	cornflower	cardinal	112–117	Fair Isle	cornflower	rain cloud
30	,,	rich purple	cardinal	118	plain	cornflower	
31	plain	rich purple		119	Fair Isle	cornflower	frolic
32–37	Fair Isle	rich purple	rain cloud	120	,,	black	frolic
38	plain	rich purple		121	plain	black	
39	Fair Isle	rich purple	black	122–127	Fair Isle	black	cardinal
40	,,	cardinal	black	128	plain	black	
41	plain	cardinal		129	Fair Isle	black	signal red
42–47	Fair Isle	cardinal	deep blue	130	,,	rich purple	signal red
48	plain	cardinal		131	plain	rich purple	
49	Fair Isle	cardinal	signal red	132–137	Fair Isle	rich purple	purple chenille
50	,,	black	signal red	138	plain	rich purple	
51	plain	black		139	Fair Isle	rich purple	frolic
52–57	Fair Isle	black	purple chenille	140	,,	deep blue	frolic
58	plain	black		141	plain	deep blue	
59	Fair Isle	black	rain cloud	142–147	Fair Isle	deep blue	cyclamen
60	,,	claret	rain cloud	148	plain	deep blue	
61	plain	claret		149	Fair Isle	deep blue	signal red
62–67	Fair Isle	claret	rich purple	150	,,	bright blue	signal red
68	plain	claret		151	plain	bright blue	
69	Fair Isle	claret	cornflower	152–157	Fair Isle	bright blue	cardinal
70	,,	deep blue	cornflower	158	plain	bright blue	
71	plain	deep blue		159	Fair Isle	bright blue	black
72–77	Fair Isle	deep blue	signal red	160	,,	rich purple	black
78	plain	deep blue		161	plain	rich purple	
79	Fair Isle	deep blue	frolic	162–167	Fair Isle	rich purple	signal red

BACK
Bring forward 140 needles to WP.
Using waste yarn cast on, and knit 6 rows.
MT–2. Using rich purple, knit 9 rows.
Insert punchcard 1 and lock on first row of patt.
Knit 1 row.
RC 000. MT. Working patt sequence as given in chart, knit to RC 10.
Make hem by picking up loops from first row in rich purple and placing on to needles.
Continuing in patt sequence as given in chart, knit to RC 124.
Shape armholes
Keeping patt sequence correct, cast off (bind off) 6 sts at beg of next 2 rows and 2 sts at beg of foll 4 rows.
RC 130. 120 sts.
Dec 1 st each end of every row until 106 sts rem, then each end of every foll alt row until 100 sts rem. RC 143.
Knit to RC 196.
Shape shoulders
Cast off (bind off) 30 sts at beg of next 2 rows. 40 sts.
Using waste yarn, knit 6 rows. Release sts from machine.

POCKET LININGS (make 2)
Bring forward 26 needles to WP.
Using rich purple, cast on using the closed edge method.
MT. RC 000. Knit to RC 30.
Using waste yarn, knit 6 rows.
Release sts from machine.

RIGHT FRONT
(Lower edge)
Bring forward 70 needles to WP.
Work as given for back to RC 41.
Place centre 26 needles into HP.
Push all needles at right of needlebed to HP.
Using waste yarn, knit 6 rows. Release sts from machine.
Return 7 needles at right to WP.
Using waste yarn, knit 6 rows. Release sts from machine.
Return 26 centre sts to WP.
Pocket border
Insert punchcard 3 and lock on first row of patt.
Set patt into memory.
Set machine for Fair Isle.
Release card, then with rich purple in feeder A, knit 1 row with purple chenille in feeder B, then 1 row with cardinal and 1 row with lacquer.
Set machine for plain knitting.
MT–2. Knit 6 rows.
Cast off (bind off) loosely.

1

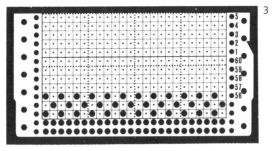

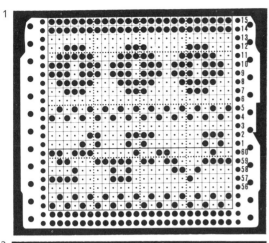

3

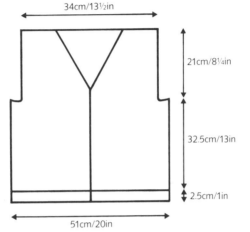

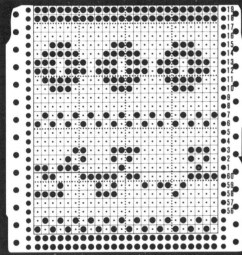

34cm/13½in

21cm/8¼in

32.5cm/13in

2.5cm/1in

51cm/20in

LEFT FRONT
(Lower edge)
Work as given for lower edge of right front.

RIGHT FRONT
(Main part)
Bring forward 3 needles at centre of machine.
Insert punchcard 1 and lock on row 3 of patt.
Using claret, cast on and knit 2 rows.
MT. RC 000. Working in patt sequence as given in chart shape as follows:
Increasing 1 st at right on next and ever foll alt row, inc 1 st at left on every row until there are 104 sts. RC 70.
Shape armhole
Dec 1 st at left and cast off (bind off) 6 sts at right on next row. 97 sts. RC 71.
Keeping right edge straight, dec 1 st at left on every foll alt row until RC 99. 83 sts.
Now continuing to dec 1 st at left on every alt row, inc 1 st at right (armhole edge) on every row to RC 130. 99 sts.
Shape shoulder and front neck
Casting off (binding off) 5 sts at left on next and every foll alt row, dec 1 st at right on next and every foll alt row until 3 sts rem. RC 162.
Cast off (bind off).

LEFT FRONT
(Main part)
Work as given for main part of right front, reversing all shaping by reading left for right and right for left.

FRONT BORDERS
Bring forward 70 needles to WP.
Carriage at left.
With RS of lower edge of right front facing, hook first 7 sts held on waste yarn on to first 7 needles, pick up first row of sts in rich purple at top of pocket lining and place

on to next 26 needles, then hook second set of 7 sts held on waste yarn and place on to rem 7 needles.
With WS facing, pick up 70 sts evenly along lower edge of main part of right front and place on to same needles.
MT + 1. Using rich purple, knit 1 row.
Cast off (bind off).
Bring forward 160 needles to WP.
With WS facing, pick up 160 sts along right front edge and place on to needles.
* Insert punchcard 1 and lock on row 14 of patt.
MT−1. Using rich purple, knit 3 rows.
Set machine for Fair Isle. Release card.
With rich purple in feeder A and bright blue in feeder B, knit 6 rows.
Set machine for plain knitting.
Knit 10 rows.
Make hem by picking up loops of first row in rich purple and placing on to needles.
Knit 1 row.
Cast off (bind off) loosely. *
Repeat for left front.

BACK NECKBAND
Bring forward 40 needles to WP.
With WS facing, pick up 40 sts held on waste yarn at back neck.
Now work as given for right front border from * to *.

ARMHOLE BORDERS
Join shoulder and neck border seams.
Bring forward 154 needles to WP.
With WS facing, pick up 154 sts evenly round armhole edge and place on to needles.
Insert punchcard 3 and lock on first row of patt.
Set patt into memory.
Knit 1 row rich purple.
Set machine for Fair Isle.
Release card, then with rich purple in feeder A, knit 1 row with purple chenille in feeder B, then 1 row with cardinal and 1 row with lacquer.
Set machine for plain knitting.
MT−2. Knit 6 rows.
Cast off (bind off) loosely.

TO MAKE UP
Join side seams. Fold armhole borders and pocket tops in half to WS and slipstitch into place. Sew pocket linings in position.

MARGARET HYNE

TOMMY WAISTCOAT

Right: Shades of red and deep pink form vertical bands against a navy background on this warm tuck stitch waistcoat.

MATERIALS
Rowan Botany 4 ply
500g/18oz in main colour A
Rowan Light Tweed
100g/4oz in each of contrast colours B, C, D and E
50g/2oz of same in contrast colour F
8 press fasteners

MEASUREMENTS
To fit bust 86–97cm/34–38in
Actual size
Bust 112cm/44in
Length 57cm/22½in

TENSION
25 sts and 36 rows to 10cm/4in worked over st st with TD at approx 9

MACHINE
Any Brother standard gauge electronic or punchcard machine with ribbing attachment or equivalent
(If ribbing attachment not available see Alternative methods of ribbing in techniques – p.123)

BACK
Bring forward 73 needles on main bed to WP. (65 needles at left of centre and 8 at right.)
Cast on with waste yarn and knit 7 rows, ending with carriage at left.
Insert punchcard (joined into a circle) and lock on first row of pattern.
RC 000. MT. Knit 1 row in A.
Set machine for tuck knitting.
MT−1. Release card and knit 30 rows in A.
Set machine for plain knitting. MT.
Bring forward 60 needles at right to WP.
Using A, cast on over the 60 needles using the closed edge method, then knit to RC 53.
Knit 2 rows B, then 17 rows A. RC 72.
MT + 1. Knit 2 rows A.
MT. Knit 1 row. RC 75.
Set machine for tuck knitting.
MT−1. Knit 30 rows C. RC 105.
Make hem as follows: using triple transfer tool, pick up loops from first of 2 rows in B and place on to needles holding sts (2 sts on each needle).
This completes the first pleated stripe.
Work second pleated stripe as follows:
* Set machine for plain knitting.
MT. Knit 20 rows in A.
Knit 2 rows B, then 17 rows A.
MT + 1. Knit 2 rows A.
MT. Knit 1 row.
Set machine for tuck knitting.
MT−1. Knit 30 rows D.
Make hem, picking up loops from first of 2 rows in B. *
RC 177.
Using first E, then F, instead of D, rep from * to * twice more. RC 321.
Centre back stripe
Set machine for plain knitting.
MT. Knit 2 rows A.
Set machine for tuck knitting.
MT−1. Knit 20 rows B.
Set machine for plain knitting.
MT. Knit 2 rows A. RC 345.
Work reversed pleated stripes as follows:
** Set machine for tuck knitting.
MT−1. Knit 30 rows F.
Set machine for plain knitting.

MT. Knit 1 row.
MT + 1. Knit 2 rows A.
MT. Knit 17 rows A, then 2 rows B.
Make hem, picking up loops from first of 30 rows in F.
Set machine for plain knitting.
MT. Knit 20 rows in A. **
This completes a reversed pleated stripe.
Using first E, then D and C, instead of F, rep from ** to ** 3 times more. RC 633.
Carriage at right.
Knit 2 rows in A.
Cast off (bind off) 60 sts at right.
Set machine for tuck knitting.
MT−1. Knit 30 rows A.
Set machine for plain knitting.
MT. Knit 1 row.
Using waste yarn, knit 6 rows. Release sts from machine.

RIGHT FRONT
Work as given for back until RC 107.
Cut off A.
Pocket
Push first 5 needles at left and 93 needles at right into HP.
Work on rem 35 sts.
RC 000. MT. Knit 120 rows in A.
Return all needles to WP. Set RC to 107.
Cont in pleated stripe patt as given for back to RC 251.
Carriage at right.
Shape neck
Cast off (bind off) 7 sts at right.
Cont in patt until RC 323.
Cast off (bind off) 18 sts at right.
Place a marker at each end of last row.
Set machine for tuck knitting.
MT−1. Knit 20 rows A.
Set machine for plain knitting.
MT. Knit 2 rows.
Set machine for tuck knitting.
MT−1. Knit 20 rows.
Make hem, picking up loops from marked row.
Cast off (bind off) loosely.

LEFT FRONT
Bring forward 108 needles on main bed to WP. (65 needles at left of centre and 43 at right.)
Cast on with waste yarn and knit 7 rows, ending with carriage at left.
Insert punchcard (joined into a circle) and lock on first row of pattern.
MT. Knit 1 row A.
Set machine for tuck knitting.
RC 000. MT−1. Knit 20 rows A.
Set machine for plain knitting.
MT. Knit 2 rows. Set machine for tuck knitting.
MT−1. Knit 20 rows. RC 42.
Make hem, picking up loops from first row in A.
Remove waste yarn.
RC 000. Carriage at right.
Set machine for plain knitting.
Shape neck
With A, cast on 18 sts at right using the closed edge method.
Knit 2 rows.
Work reversed pleated stripes as follows:
Set machine for tuck knitting.
MT−1. Knit 30 rows F.
Set machine for plain knitting.
MT. Knit 1 row.
MT + 1. Knit 2 rows A.

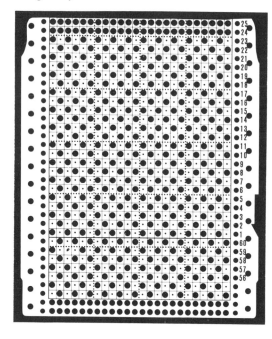

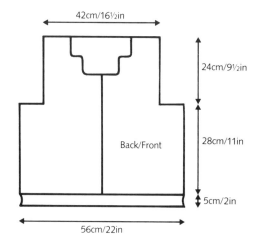

42cm/16½in

24cm/9½in

Back/Front

28cm/11in

5cm/2in

56cm/22in

MT. Knit 17 rows A, then 2 rows B.
Make hem, picking up loops from first of 30 rows in F.
Set machine for plain knitting.
MT. Knit 18 rows in A.
With A, cast on 7 sts at right using the closed edge method. 133 sts.
** Knit 2 rows A.
Set machine for tuck knitting.
MT−1. Knit 30 rows E.
Set machine for plan knitting.
MT. Knit 1 row.
MT + 1. Knit 2 rows A.
MT. Knit 17 rows A, then 2 rows B.
Make hem, picking up loops from first of 30 rows in F.
Set machine for plain knitting.
MT. Knit 18 rows in A. **
RC 144. Using D instead of E, rep from ** to **. RC 216. Cut off A.
Pocket
Push first 5 needles at left and 93 needles at right into HP.
Work on rem 35 sts.
RC 000. MT. Knit 120 rows in A.
Return all needles to WP. Set RC to 216.
Using C instead of E, rep from ** to **. RC 288.
Knit 2 rows A.
Carriage at right.
Cast off (bind off) 60 sts at right.
Set machine for tuck knitting.
MT−1. Knit 30 rows A.

Set machine for plain knitting.
MT. Knit 1 row.
Using waste yarn, knit 6 rows. Release sts from machine.

SHOULDER INSETS
Bring forward 32 needles on main bed to WP.
With WS of front facing, pick up 32 sts (through all thicknesses) along shoulder edge and place on to needles in WP.
MT−1. Knit 2 rows D, then 4 rows A.
Make hem by picking up loops from first row in A.
Knit 2 rows D.
Using waste yarn, knit 6 rows. Release sts from machine.
With RS of front facing, pick up sts from last row in A and hook on to needles. Remove waste yarn.
With WS of back facing, pick up 32 sts (through all thicknesses) of corresponding shoulder, matching colours, and place on to same needles.
MT + 1. Knit 1 row A.
Cast off (bind off).

ARMHOLE BORDERS
Bring forward 116 needles on main bed to WP.
Using waste yarn, cast on and knit 6 rows. Set machine for tuck knitting.
RC 000. MT−1. Knit 5 rows A.
Winding yarn round first needle in HP at beg of every row, push 4 needles into HP at opposite end to carriage on every row until 36 sts rem.
Push 4 needles at opposite end to carriage back into WP on every row until all needles in WP.
Make hem, picking up first row worked in A. Set machine for plain knitting.
MT. Knit 1 row A. Carriage at left.
With WS of armhole facing, pick up 116 sts along armhole edge and place on to needles.
MT + 1. Knit 1 row A.
Cast off (bind off) loosely.

WELT
Bring forward 120 needles on each bed to WP.
Arrange needles for 1 × 1 rib.
Using A cast on, ending with carriage at right.
MT−3, knit 41 rows. Carriage at left.
Transfer all sts to main bed.
With WS of work facing, pick up 60 sts along lower edge of right front and back to centre back and place on to needles holding welt sts.
MT + 1. Knit 1 row.
Cast off (bind off) loosely.
Make a second welt in the same way, attaching to second half of back and left front.

NECKBAND
Bring forward 100 needles on each bed to WP.
Arrange needles for 1 × 1 rib.
Using A cast on, ending with carriage at right.
MT−3, knit 19 rows. Carriage at left.
Transfer all sts to main bed.
With WS of back facing, pick up 100 sts round neck edge and place on to needles holding neckband.
MT + 1. Knit 1 row. Cast off (bind off) loosely.

TO MAKE UP
With RS of back facing, replace sts of side seam on to needles and remove waste yarn. Push sts back behind latches.
With WS of front facing, place corresponding sts of side seam on to same needles holding sts of back, leaving the sts in the hooks, then remove waste yarn.
Carefully push back each needle, so pulling sts of front through sts of back. Using A, cast off (bind off) sts.
Repeat on second side seam.
Fold neckband in half to WS and slipstitch down.
Join seam at centre back welt, then fold welt in half to Ws and slipstitch in position. Sew on press fasteners to front borders. Join row ends of pocket, then sew fold of pocket into place behind pleat to secure. Stitch down pleats for about 20cm/8in at top.

MARGARET HYNE

TOMMY JACKET

MATERIALS
Rowan Botany 4 ply
750g/27oz in main colour A (black 62)
Rowan Light Tweed
100g/4oz of contrast colours B (bracken 204), C (charcoal 210), D (grey 209) and E (silver 208)
50g/2oz of contrast colour F (pebble 203)
5 buttons
4 press fasteners

MEASUREMENTS
To fit bust 86–107cm/34–42in
Actual size
Bust 124cm/49in
Length 66cm/26in
Sleeve seam 51cm/20¼in

TENSION
25 sts and 36 rows to 10cm/4in worked over st st with TD at approx 9

MACHINE
Any Brother standard gauge electronic or punchcard machine with ribbing attachment or equivalent
(If ribbing attachment not available see Alternative methods of ribbing in techniques – p.123)

BACK
Bring forward 78 needles on main bed to WP. (70 needles at left of centre and 8 at right.)
Cast on with waste yarn and knit 7 rows, ending with carriage at left.
Insert punchcard (joined into a circle) and lock on first row of pattern.
RC 000. MT. Knit 1 row in A.
Set machine for tuck knitting.
MT−1. Release card and knit 30 rows in A.
Set machine for plain knitting. MT.
Bring forward 64 needles at right to WP.
Using A, cast on over the 64 needles, then knit to RC 53.
Knit 2 rows B, then 17 rows A. RC 72.
MT + 1. Knit 2 rows A.
MT. Knit 1 row. RC 75.
Set machine for tuck knitting.
MT−1. Knit 30 rows C. RC 105.
Make hem as follows: using triple transfer tool, pick up loops from first of 2 rows in B and place on to needles holding sts (2 sts on each needle).
This completes the first pleated stripe.
Work second pleated stripe as follows:
* Set machine for plain knitting.
MT. Knit 20 rows in A.
Knit 2 rows B, then 17 rows A.
MT + 1. Knit 2 rows A.
MT. Knit 1 row.
Set machine for tuck knitting.
MT−1. Knit 30 rows D.
Make hem, picking up loops from first of 2 rows in B. *
RC 177.
Using first E, then F, instead of D, rep from * to * twice more. RC 321.

Centre back stripe
Set machine for plain knitting.
MT. Knit 2 rows A.
Set machine for tuck knitting.
MT−1. Knit 20 rows B.
Set machine for plain knitting.
MT. Knit 2 rows A.
Work reversed pleated stripes as follows:
** Set machine for tuck knitting.

MT−1. Knit 30 rows F.
Set machine for plain knitting.
MT. Knit 1 row.
MT + 1. Knit 2 rows A.
MT. Knit 17 rows A, then 2 rows B.
Make hem, picking up loops from first of 30 rows in F.
Set machine for plain knitting.
MT. Knit 20 rows in A. **
This completes a reversed pleated stripe.
Using first E, then D and C, instead of F, rep from ** to ** 3 times more. RC 633.
Carriage at right.
Knit 2 rows in A.
Cast off (bind off) 64 sts at right.
Set machine for tuck knitting.
MT−1. Knit 30 rows A.
Set machine for plain knitting.
MT. Knit 1 row.
Using waste yarn, knit 6 rows. Release sts from machine.

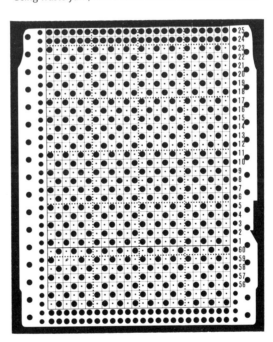

RIGHT FRONT
Work as given for back until RC 107.
Cut off A.
Pocket
Push first 5 needles at left and 102 needles at right into HP.
Work on rem 35 sts.
RC 000. MT. Knit 120 rows in A.
Return all needles to WP. Set RC to 107.
Cont in pleated stripe patt as given for back to RC 251.
Carriage at right.
Shape neck
Cast off (bind off) 6 sts at right.
Cont in patt until RC 323.
Cast off (bind off) 18 sts at right.
Set machine for tuck knitting.
MT−1. Knit 59 rows A. RC 382.
Set machine for plain knitting.
Make buttonholes over needles as follows:
Counting from left, miss the first 3 needles.
* Using a short length of A cast off (bind off) the next 3 sts, then using the same length of yarn, cast on 3 sts

manually over these 3 needles *. Miss the next 33 needles, rep from * to *, miss the next 33 needles, rep from * to *, miss the next 34 needles, rep from * to *, miss final 3 needles at right.
MT−2. Knit 7 rows A.
MT. Knit 2 rows.
MT−2. Knit 8 rows.
Make hem, picking up loops from first of 7 rows in A.
Cast off (bind off) loosely.

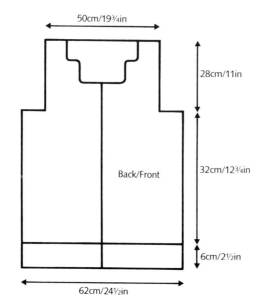

50cm/19¾in

28cm/11in

Back/Front

32cm/12¾in

6cm/2½in

62cm/24½in

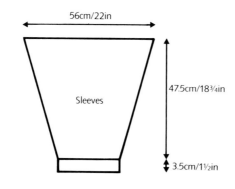

56cm/22in

Sleeves

47.5cm/18¾in

3.5cm/1½in

LEFT FRONT
Bring forward 118 needles on main bed to WP. (70 needles at left of centre and 48 at right.)
Cast on with waste yarn and knit 6 rows, ending with carriage at right.
Insert punchcard (joined into a circle) and lock on first row of pattern.
RC 000. MT−2. Knit 8 rows A.
MT. Knit 2 rows.
MT−2. Knit 7 rows. RC 17.
Make hem, picking up loops from first row in A.
Remove waste yarn.
RC 000. Work reversed pleated stripes as follows:
Set machine for tuck knitting.
MT−1. Knit 59 rows A.
Carriage at right.
Set machine for plain knitting.
Shape neck
With A, cast on 18 sts at right using the closed edge method.
Knit 2 rows.
Set machine for tuck knitting.
MT−1. Knit 30 rows F.
Set machine for plain knitting.
MT. Knit 1 row.
MT + 1. Knit 2 rows A.
MT. Knit 17 rows A, then 2 rows B.

Make hem, picking up loops from first of 30 rows in F.
Set machine for plain knitting.
MT. Knit 18 rows in A.
This completes a reversed pleated stripe.
With A, cast on 6 sts at right using the closed edge method. 142 sts.
** Knit 2 rows A.
Set machine for tuck knitting.
MT−1. Knit 30 rows E.
Set machine for plain knitting.
MT. Knit 1 row.
MT + 1. Knit 2 rows A.
MT. Knit 17 rows A, then 2 rows B.
Make hem, picking up loops from first of 30 rows in E.
Set machine for plain knitting.
MT. Knit 18 rows in A. **
Using D instead of E, rep from ** to **. RC 275.
Cut off A.
Pocket
Push first 5 needles at left and 102 needles at right into HP.
Work on rem 35 sts.
RC 000. MT. Knit 120 rows in A.
Return all needles to WP. Set RC to 275.
Using C instead of E, rep from ** to **. RC 347.
Carriage at right.
Knit 2 rows A.
Cast off (bind off) 64 sts at right.
Set machine for tuck knitting.
MT−1. Knit 30 rows A. RC 379.
Set machine for plain knitting.
MT. Knit 1 row.
Using waste yarn, knit 6 rows. Release sts from machine.

SLEEVES
Bring forward 120 needles on main bed to WP.
Using waste yarn, cast on and knit 6 rows.
Insert punchcard (joined into a circle) and lock on first row of pattern.
RC 000. MT−1. Knit 1 row in A and 1 row in B.
Set machine for tuck knitting.
MT−1. Release card and knit 12 rows in A.
Winding yarn round first needle in HP, push 6 needles to HP at opposite end to carriage on next 14 rows. RC 28. 36 needles left in WP.
Return 6 needles to WP at opposite end to carriage on next 14 rows. RC 42.
Set machine for plain knitting.
MT. Knit 6 rows A. RC 48.
Make hem, picking up loops from first row in B.
RC 000. Set machine for tuck knitting.
MT−1. Dec 1 st each end of every 14 rows until 80 sts rem. RC 281.
Knit to RC 290.
Cuff
Set machine for plain knitting.
MT−1. Knit 14 rows A.
MT + 1. Knit 2 rows A.
MT−1. Knit 14 rows A.
Make hem, picking up loops from first row of cuff.
MT + 1. Knit 1 row A.
Cast off (bind off) loosely.

SHOULDER INSETS
Bring forward 32 needles on main bed to WP.
With WS of front facing, pick up 32 sts (through all thicknesses) along shoulder edge and place on to needles in WP.
MT−1. Knit 2 rows D, then 4 rows A.
Make hem by picking up loops from first row in A.
Knit 2 rows D.
Using waste yarn, knit 6 rows. Release sts from machine.
With RS of front facing, pick up sts from last row in A and hook on to needles. Remove waste yarn.
With WS of back facing, pick up 32 sts (through all thicknesses) of corresponding shoulder, matching colours, and place on to same needles.
MT + . Knit 1 row A.
Cast off (bind off).

WELT

Bring forward 150 needles on each bed to WP.
Arrange needles for 1 × 1 rib.
Using A cast on, ending with carriage at right.
MT−3, knit 65 rows.
Carriage at left.
Transfer all sts to main bed.
With WS of work facing, pick up 60 sts along lower edge of right front to centre of lower edge of back and place on to needles holding welt sts.
MT + 1. Knit 1 row. Cast off (bind off) loosely.
Make a second welt in the same way, attaching to second half of back and left front.

COLLAR

Bring foward 115 needles on each bed to WP.
Arrange needles for 1 × 1 rib.
Using A cast on, ending with carriage at right.
MT−3, knit 70 rows.
Cast off (bind off) loosely, or leave sts on waste yarn and back stitch down when sewing collar in place.

TO MAKE UP

With RS of back facing, replace sts of side seam on to needles and remove waste yarn. Push sts back behind latches.
With WS of front facing, place corresponding sts of side seam on to same needles holding sts of back, leaving the sts in the hooks, then remove waste yarn.
Carefully push back each needle, so pulling sts of front through sts of back. Using A, cast off (bind off) sts.
Repeat on second side seam.
Fold collar in half and slipstitch each edge into place, enclosing shaped front edges to form a round neck. Fold sleeves in half lengthwise, then placing folds to shoulder seams, sew into position. Roll hem at top of sleeves and slipstitch into place to form shoulder border. Join sleeve seams. Join seam at centre back welt, then fold welt in half to WS and slipstitch in position. Make a button loop at top of collar, then sew on buttons to correspond with buttonholes. Sew on press fasteners to underside of double breasted opening. Join row ends of pocket, then sew fold of pocket into place behind pleat to secure. Stitch down pleats for about 20cm/8in at top.

Above: The vertical pleats and sleeves are all knitted in a one by one tuck stitch, producing a thick fabric which looks like rib.

RIBBED SHIRT

MATERIALS
Rowan Botany 4 ply
900 (925, 950) g/32 (33, 34) oz

MEASUREMENTS
To fit bust 81–86 (91-97, 102–107) cm/32–34 (36–38, 40–42) in
Actual size
Bust 104 (116, 126) cm/41 (45½, 49½) in
Length 77 (78, 79) cm/30½ (31, 31½) in
Sleeve seam 47cm/18½in
5 buttons

TENSION
56 sts (28 sts on each bed) and 42 rows to 10cm/4in worked over full needle rib with TD at approx 6

MACHINE
Any Brother standard gauge electronic or punchcard machine with ribbing attachment or equivalent

BACK
(Knited from shoulders down.)
Bring forward 146 (162, 178) needles on each bed to WP. Arrange needles for full needle rib.
Cast on for shoulders, ending with carriage at right.
Place a marker on the 34th st each side of centre to denote back neck.
RC 000. MT. Knit to RC 126.
Place a marker each end of last row to denote armholes.
Knit to RC 254.
** Shape lower edge
Dec 1 st from each bed at beg of next 40 rows. RC 294
106 (122, 138) sts on each bed.
Dec 1st from each bed at each end of next 26 (28, 30) rows. RC 324. 54 (66, 78) sts on each bed.
Cast off (bind off) 6 sts from each bed at beg of next 4 (6, 8) rows. RC 324 (328, 332). 30 sts on each bed.
Cast off (bind off) in rib (using the latch tool). **

FRONT
(Knitted from shoulders down.)
Beginning at the 73rd (81st, 89th) needle to left of centre, bring foward 39 (47, 55) needles on each bed to WP. Arrange needles for full needle rib.
Cast on for shoulder, ending with carriage at right.
Knit to RC 12.
Shape neck
Bring forward 1 needle at right on each bed on every row until there are 73 (81, 89) needles in WP on each bed. RC 46.
Knit straight to RC 126.
Place a marker at left edge of last row to denote armhole.
Knit straight to RC 182.
Using waste yarn, knit all sts by hand, leaving long loops so that needles are in NWP.
Beginning at the 73rd (81st, 89th) needle to right of centre, bring foward 39 (47, 55) needles on each bed to WP. Arrange needles for full needle rib.
Cast on for shoulder, ending with carriage at right.
Knit to RC 12.
Shape neck
Bring forward 1 needle at left on each bed on every row until there are 73 (81, 89) needles in WP on each bed. RC 46.
Knit straight to RC 126.
Place a marker at right edge of last row to denote armhole.
Knit straight to RC 182.

Left: Using every needle instead of every alternate needle, when working this ribbed shirt, produces a warm, thick fabric ideal for outdoor wear.

Right: This Ribbed Shirt by Erika Knight can easily be made longer or shorter to suit individual tastes; but remember the yarn amounts will differ.

Gently pulling waste yarn, bring all needles at left into WP. 146 (162, 178) sts on each bed.
Knit to RC 254.
Now shape lower edge as given for back from ** to **

SLEEVES
(Knitted from top down.)
Bring forward 168 needles on each bed to WP.
Arrange needles for full needle rib.
Cast on for top edge, ending with carriage at right.
RC 000. MT. Dec 1 st, on each bed, at each end of every 6th row until 112 sts rem on each bed.
RC 168.
Knit to RC 200.
Cast off (bind off) in rib (using the latch tool).

BUTTON BORDER
Bring forward 30 needles on each bed to WP (15 needles each side of centre 0). Arrange needles for full needle rib.
Cast on, ending with carriage at right.
RC 000. MT. Knit to RC 120.
Cast off (bind off) in rib.

BUTTONHOLE BORDER
Work as given for button border, making buttonholes at RC 15, 36, 57, 78 and 99 as follows:
Buttonhole
Using a short length of waste yarn knit by hand the sts on needles 7, 8 and 9 each side of centre on both beds. Leave needles in WP to be knitted in main yarn on next row.

POCKETS
Bring forward 59 needles on each bed to WP. Arrange needles for 2 × 2 rib.
Cast on, ending with carriage at right.
RC 000. MT. Knit to RC 68. Cast off (bind off).

COLLAR
Bring forward 197 needles on each bed to WP.
Arrange needles for 2 × 2 rib.
Cast on, ending with carriage at right.
RC 000. MT. Knit to RC 76.
Cast off (bind off).

TO MAKE UP
Fold button and buttonhole borders in half and neatly slipstitch into position down centre front edges,

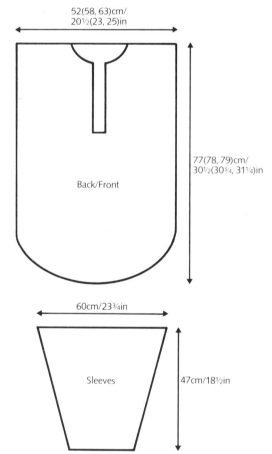

52(58, 63)cm/
20½(23, 25)in

Back/Front

77(78, 79)cm/
30½(30¾, 31¼)in

60cm/23¾in

Sleeves

47cm/18½in

27cm/10¾in

enclosing front edges by approx 2cm/½in. Removing waste yarn carefully and sewing through both thicknesses, neaten buttonholes. Join shoulder seams. Placing edges of collar halfway along button and buttonhole borders, sew on collar. Fold sleeves in half lengthwise, then placing folds to shoulder seams, sew into position. Join side and sleeve seams. Folding top 3cm/1¼in to right side, sew on pockets. Sew on buttons.

ERIKA KNIGHT

LACE COLLARED BLOUSE

MATERIALS
Either Rowan Sea Breeze 4 ply
625 (650, 675) g/22 (23, 24) oz
Or Rowan Botany 4 ply
525 (550, 575) g/19 (20, 21) oz
10 small buttons
A pair of 3mm (US2) knitting needles for hand knitted collar (optional)

MEASUREMENTS
To fit bust 81–86 (91–97, 102–107) cm/32–34 (36–38, 40–42) in
Actual size
Bust 96 (106, 116) cm/38 (42, 46) in
Length 74 cm/29 in
Sleeve seam 44 cm/17½ in

TENSION
32 sts and 45 rows to 10 cm/4 in worked over st st with TD at approx 6

MACHINE
Any Brother standard gauge machine with ribbing attachment

BACK
Bring forward 154 (168, 186) needles on each bed to WP. Arrange needles for 1 × 1 rib.
Cast on, ending with carriage at right.
MT–3, knit 16 rows.
Transfer all sts to main bed.
RC 000. MT.
Knit to RC 126.
Waist rib
Arrange needles for 1 × 1 rib.
RC 000. MT–3, knit 40 rows.
Transfer all sts to main bed.
RC 000. MT.
Knit to RC 36.
Mark each end of last row with a piece of coloured thread to denote armholes.
Knit to RC 134.
Shape neck
Using a spare length of yarn, cast off (bind off) centre 46 (48, 50) sts.
Push all needles at left of needlebed to HP.
Work on first side of neck as follows:
Dec 1 st at neck edge on next and foll 3 alt rows.
Knit 1 row. 50 (56, 62) sts.
RC 142. Cast off (bind off).
Return needles at left to WP.
Complete to match first side of neck, reversing all shaping.

LEFT FRONT
Bring forward 73 (80, 89) needles on each bed to WP. Arrange needles for 1 × 1 rib.
Cast on, ending with carriage at right.
MT–3, knit 16 rows.
Transfer all sts to main bed.
RC 000. MT.
Knit to RC 126.
Waist rib
Arrange needles for 1 × 1 rib.
RC 000. MT–3, knit 40 rows.
Transfer all sts to main bed.
RC 000. MT.
Knit to RC 36.
Mark left hand edge with a piece of coloured thread to denote armhole.

Knit to RC 114. Carriage at right.
(For right front knit to RC 115 to end with carriage at left.)
Shape neck
Cast off (bind off) 4 sts at beg of next row and 3 sts at beg of foll alt row.
Dec 1 st at neck edge on every row until 50 (56, 62) sts rem.
Knit to RC 142. Cast off (bind off).

RIGHT FRONT
Work as given for left front, noting the exception given in brackets.

SLEEVES
Bring forward 76 needles on each bed to WP. Arrange needles for 1 × 1 rib.
Cast on, ending with carriage at right.
MT–3, knit 40 rows.
RC 000. MT.
Inc 1 st each end of every 4th row until there are 126 sts, then on every foll 3rd row until there are 154 sts. RC 143.
Knit to RC 152.
Cast off (bind off).

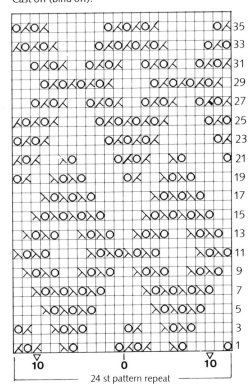

24 st pattern repeat

KEY

⊙
Transfer st to adjacent needle leaving empty needle in WP

⊠
st transferred from needle on right (2 sts on needle)

⊡
st transferred from needle on left (2 sts on needle)

COLLAR
(Machine knit lace version for machines without a lace carriage)
Bring forward 150 needles on main bed.
Cast on with waste yarn and knit 6 rows.
Change to main yarn.
RC 000. MT. Knit 2 rows.
Work lace
Working from row 1 of chart, transfer marked sts on to

the adjacent needles, repeating pattern as necessary over needles.
Knit 2 rows.
Working from row 3 of chart, transfer marked sts on to the adjacent needles.
Knit 2 rows.
Cont in this way until RC 60.
Folding collar in half, pick up sts of first row in main yarn and place on to needles holding sts.
Remove waste yarn.
MT−1. Knit 1 row.
Cast off (bind off).

Right: The collar and pocket top on this blouse have been hand knitted, but instructions are given for a machine knitted version.

COLLAR

(Machine knit lace version for machines with a lace carriage)
Bring forward 150 needles on main bed.
Cast on with waste yarn and knit 6 rows.
Change to main yarn.
Insert punchcards 1 and 2 (joined together) and lock on first row.
RC 000. MT. Knit 2 rows.
Set machine for lace knitting.
Transfering sts with lace carriage, knit to RC 60.
Folding collar in half, pick up sts of first row in main yarn and place on to needles holding sts.
Remove waste yarn.
MT + 1. Knit 1 row.
Cast off (bind off).

POCKET

(Machine knit lace version for machines without a lace carriage)
Bring forward 28 needles on main bed.
Cast on using the closed edge method.
RC 000. MT. Knit to RC 26.
Work lace
Working from row 1 of chart, transfer marked sts on to the adjacent needles.
Knit 2 rows.
Working from row 3 of chart, transfer marked sts on to the adjacent needles.
Knit 2 rows.
Cont in this way until RC 84.
Cast off (bind off).

POCKET

(Machine knit lace version for machines with a lace carriage)
Bring forward 28 needles on main bed.
Cast on using the closed edge method.

Below: Close up detail of the machine knitted pocket top.

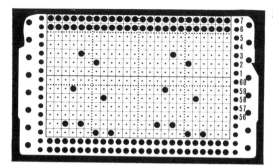

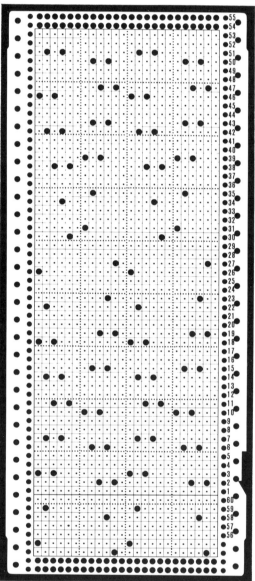

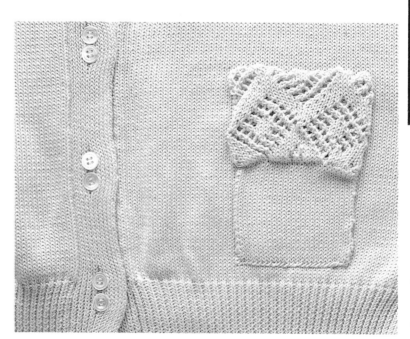

Insert punchcards 1 and 2 (joined together) and lock on first row.
RC 000. MT. Knit to RC 26.
Set machine for lace knitting.
Transfering sts with lace carriage, knit to RC 84.
Cast off (bind off).

POCKET

(Hand knit lace version)
Bring forward 28 needles on main bed.
Cast on using the closed edge method.
RC 000. MT. Knit to RC. 26.
Cast off (bind off).

HAND KNIT LACE POCKET TOP

Using 3mm (US2) needles cast on 17 sts.
Work in patt as follows:

Left: Close up detail of the hand knitted collar.

Row 1 K2, yf, k3, yf, k2 tog, [pl, k1] 5 times.
Row 2 Wind yarn round needle to make a st, k2 tog, [k1, p1] 3 times, k1, k2 tog, yf, k5, yf, k2.
Row 3 K2, yf, k1, k2 tog, yf, k1, yf, k2 tog, k1, yf, k2 tog, [p1, k1] 4 times.
Row 4 Wind yarn round needle to make a st, k2 tog, [k1, p1] twice, k1, [k2 tog, yf, k1] twice, k2, yf, k2 tog, k1, yf, k2.
Row 5 K2, yf, k1, k2 tog, yf, k5, yf, k2 tog, k1, yf, k2 tog, [p1, k1] 3 times.
Row 6 Wind yarn round needle to make a st, k2 tog, k1, p1, k1, [k2 tog, yf, k1] twice, k6, yf, k2 tog, k1, yf, k2.
Row 7 [K2 tog, k1, yf] twice, k2 tog, k3, [k2 tog, yf, k1] twice, [p1, k1] 3 times.
Row 8 Wind yarn round needle to make a st, k2 tog, [k1, p1] 3 times, yon, k2 tog, k1, yf, k2 tog, [k1, k2 tog, yf] twice, k1, k2 tog.
Row 9 [K2 tog, k1, yf] twice, k3 tog, yf, k1, k2 tog, yf, [k1, p1] 4 times, k1.
Row 10 Wind yarn round needle to make a st, k2 tog, [k1, p1] 4 times, yon, k2 tog, k3, k2 tog, yf, k1, k2 tog.
Row 11 K2 tog, k1, yf, k2 tog, k1, k2 tog, yf, [k1, p1] 5 times, k1.
Row 12 Wind yarn round needle to make a st, k2 tog, [k1, p1] 5 times, yon, k3 tog, yf, k1, k2 tog.
These 12 rows form the patt.
Cont in patt until lace is long enough to fit along top of pocket.
Cast off (bind off).

HAND KNIT LACE COLLAR
Work as given for hand knit lace pocket top until collar is long enough to fit round neck.
Cast off (bind off).

BUTTON BORDER
Bring forward 20 needles on each bed to WP. Arrange needles for 1 × 1 rib.
Cast on, ending with carriage at right.
MT−3, knit 220 rows. Cast off (bind off).

BUTTONHOLE BORDER
Work as given for button border, working buttonholes at RC 6, 11, 29, 34, 52, 57, 75, 80, 98, and 103 as follows:
Buttonhole
Transfer the 10th st in from the right on to the 9th needle at right, then transfer the 10th st from left on to the 9th needle at left.
Leave empty needles in WP.
Knit the row.

TO MAKE UP
Join shoulder seams.
Folds sleeves in half lengthwise, then placing folds to shoulder seams, sew into position.
Join side and sleeve seams. Sew on button and buttonhole borders. Sew on buttons.
Sew on lace collar at neck, beginning and ending halfway across button and buttonhole borders.
Sew hand knitted lace pocket top into position.
Fold machine knitted lace pocket top in half to WS and slipstitch into place.
Sew on pocket.

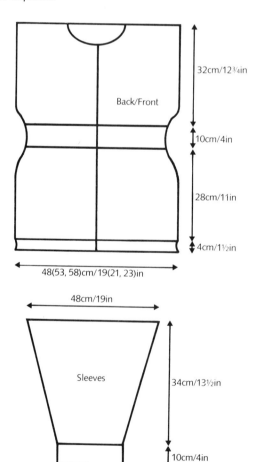

ALISON TAYLOR

HERALDIC SWEATER

MATERIALS
Rowan Lightweight DK
700 (725, 750) g/25 (26, 27) oz in main colour A
50g/2oz in contrast colour B
Rowan Fine Cotton Chenille
100g/4oz in contrast colour C
100g/4oz in contrast colour D

MEASUREMENTS
To fit chest 107 (112, 117) cm/42 (44, 46) in
Actual size
Chest 136 (140, 144) cm/53½ (55, 56½) in
Length to centre back neck 68cm/27in
Sleeve seam 48cm/19in

TENSION
26 sts and 35 rows to 10cm/4in worked over st st with
TD at approx 10

MACHINE
Any Brother standard gauge electronic or punchcard
machine with ribbing attachment or equivalent
(If ribbing attachment not available see Alternative
methods of ribbing in techniques – p.123)

FRONT
Bring forward 178 (184, 188) needles on each bed to
WP. Arrange needles for 1 × 1 rib.
Using A cast on, ending with carriage at right.
MT−3, knit 2 rows B, 2 rows A, 2 rows B, then 30 rows
A.
Transfer all sts to main bed.
RC 000. MT. Using A, knit 1 row.
Transfer sts marked on row 2 of chart to the adjacent
needle. Push empty needles back into NWP.
Knit to RC 8.
Using 2 triple transfer tools, take 3 sts on to each, where
marked on chart for cable, and cross left over right.
Replace sts on to needles and continue knitting to RC
16.
Work second row of cables, then knit to RC 23.
Bring needles pushed to NWP at centre cable back into
WP.
Pick up the loops of the sts below the sts on adjacent
needles and place on to empty needles.
Insert punchcard of lion motif and lock on first row of
pattern.
Knit 1 row. RC 24.
Set machine for single motif over centre 24 sts as shown
in chart.
Release card.
Working single motif in C, cont to work cable patt as
shown on chart until RC 74.
Set machine for plain knitting and remove punchcard.
Knit 1 row.
Transfer sts marked on chart for centre cable to the
adjacent needle. Push needles back into NWP.
Now cont in patt from chart, placing single motifs and
cables as shown, and working shaping for raglans until
RC 203.
Shape neck
Place centre 28 needles into HP.
Push all needles at right of needlebed to HP.
Work on first side of neck as follows:
Decreasing 1 st at neck edge on every row, cont to dec
at raglan edge as shown on chart until 1 st rem.
Fasten off.
Return 28 centre sts to WP. RC 203.
Using waste yarn, knit 6 rows. Release sts from machine.
Return needles at right to WP.

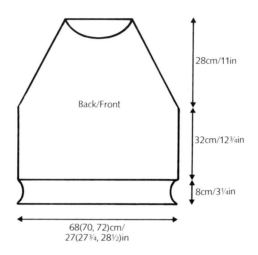

Back/Front

28cm/11in

32cm/12¾in

8cm/3¼in

68(70, 72)cm/
27(27¾, 28½)in

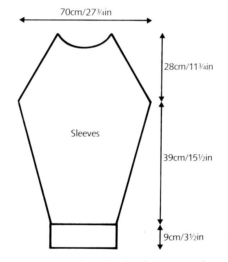

70cm/27¾in

28cm/11¾in

Sleeves

39cm/15½in

9cm/3½in

Complete to match first side of neck, reversing all
shaping.

BACK
Working cables only instead of single motifs, work as
given for front until RC 203.
Cont to dec at raglan edge as shown on chart until 32 sts
rem.
Using waste yarn, knit 6 rows. Release sts from machine.

RIGHT SLEEVE
Bring forward 92 needles on each bed to WP. Arrange
needles for 1 × 1.
Using A cast on, ending with carriage at right.
MT−3, knit 2 rows B, 2 rows A, 2 rows B, then 30 rows
A.
Transfer all sts to main bed.
RC 000. MT. Using A, knit 1 row.
Transfer sts marked on row 2 of chart to the adjacent
needle. Push empty needles back into NWP.
Cont in patt from chart, placing single motif and shaping
sides and raglans as shown, to RC 227.
Place 30 needles at right of bed into HP.
Cont to dec each side over rem sts, as shown on chart,
until 1 st rem.

KEY

Transfer st to adjacent needle and leave empty needle in NWP

Bring needle in NWP back into WP

Work cable

Work Lion motif in C

Work Bird motif in D

KEY

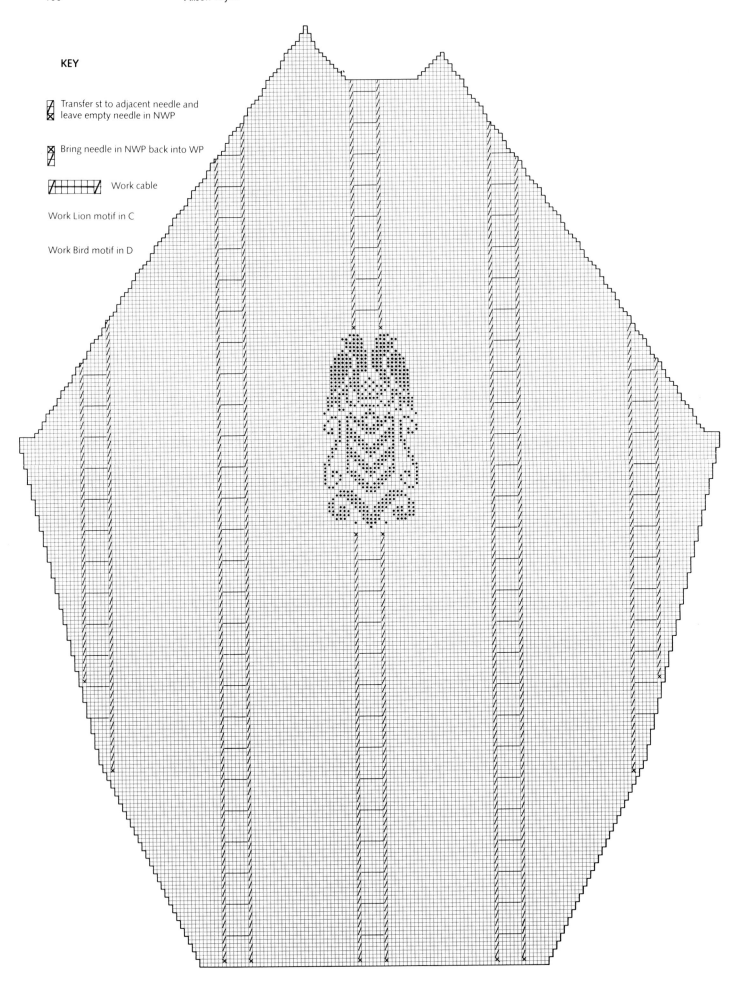

Transfer st to adjacent needle and
leave empty needle in NWP

Bring needle in NWP back into WP

Work cable

Work Lion motif in C

Work Bird motif in D

Fasten off.
Return 19 sts at left of rem sts to WP.
Using waste yarn, knit 6 rows. Release sts from machine.
Return needles at right to WP.
Cont to dec each side over rem sts, as shown on chart,
until 1 st rem.
Fasten off.

LEFT SLEEVE
Work as given for right sleeve, reversing all shaping.

NECKBAND
Bring forward 184 needles on each bed to WP.
Arrange needles for 1 × 1 rib.
Using A cast on, ending with carriage at right.
MT-3, knit 32 rows A, 2 rows B, 2 rows A, 2 rows B,
then 16 rows A. RC 54.
Using waste yarn, knit 6 rows. Release sts from machine.

TO MAKE UP
Join raglan and neckband seams. Unravelling waste yarn
as required, backstitch neckband in place round neck
edge, taking care to stitch through each stitch. Fold
neckband in half to WS, then slipstitch into place. Join
side and sleeve seams.

Above: Leave out the stripes on the cuffs, welt and neckband of the Heraldic Sweater to give a more sophisticated look.

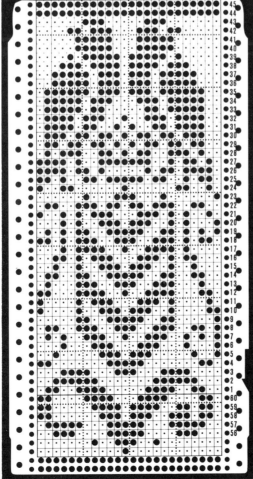

Bird motif

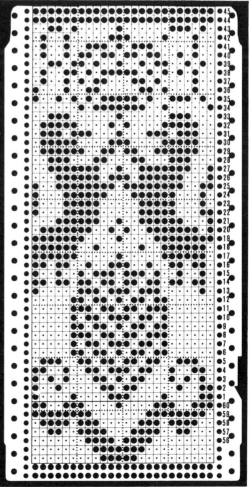

Lion motif

ALISON TAYLOR

HERRINGBONE JERSEY

Right: Stripes are worked on the cuffs, welt and neckband, picking out the colours of the slip stitch and Fair Isle pattern.

MATERIALS
Rowan Botany 4 ply
300 (325, 350, 375) g/11 (12, 13, 14) oz in airforce blue (shade 54)
100g/4oz in navy (shade 97)
75g/3oz in brown (shade 80)
100g/4oz in black (shade 62)
100g/4oz in purple (shade 99)
100g/4oz in rust (shade 71)
Rowan Fine Fleck Tweed
100g/4oz in airforce blue (shade 54)
100g/4 oz in navy (shade 97)
Rowan Light Tweed
50g/2oz in earth (shade 206)
Rowan Fine Cotton Chenille
50g/2 oz in mole (shade 380)
100g/4oz in black (shade 377)

MEASUREMENTS
To fit chest/bust 107 (112, 117, 122) cm/42 (44, 46, 48) in
Actual size
Chest/bust 110 (128, 134, 140) cm/43¼ (50½, 52¾, 55) in
Length 75 (75, 77, 77) cm/29½ (29½, 30¼, 30¼) in
Sleeve seam 53cm/21in

TENSION
29 sts and 61 rows to 10cm/4in worked over slip patt with TD at approx 8

MACHINE
Any Brother standard guage electronic or punchcard machine with ribbing attachment or equivalent
(If ribbing attachment not available see Alternative methods of ribbing in techniques – p.123)

PATTERN SEQUENCE FOR BACK AND FRONT

ROWS	PATTERN SETTING	COLOUR IN FEEDER A	COLOUR IN FEEDER B
Note: The yarns are all Botany unless the colour is followed by 'tweed' or 'chenille'. Join punchcards 1 and 2 together, then join into a circle to form 82 rows of patt beginning at row 1 on punchcard 1.			
4th size only Set to row 65 of patt			
9 rows	Fair Isle	airforce blue	navy
3rd and 4th size only Set on row 74 of patt			
9 rows	Fair Isle	airforce blue	brown
2nd, 3rd and 4th sizes only Set to row 1 of patt			
1 row	slip	airforce blue	
8 rows	,,	black tweed	
1 row	,,	airforce blue	
8 rows	,,	rust	
1 row	,,	airforce blue	
8 rows	,,	black	
All sizes ** Set to row 28 of patt			
1 row	,,	airforce blue	
8 rows	,,	mole chenille	
1 row	,,	airforce blue	
8 rows	,,	black	
1 row	,,	airforce blue	
8 rows	,,	rust	
1 row	,,	airforce blue	

ROWS	PATTERN SETTING	COLOUR IN FEEDER A	COLOUR IN FEEDER B
8 rows	,,	black tweed	
1 row	,,	airforce blue	
9 rows	Fair Isle	airforce blue	brown
9 rows	,,	airforce blue	navy
1 row	slip	airforce blue	
8 rows	,,	black chenille	
1 row	,,	airforce blue	
8 rows	,,	airforce blue tweed	
1 row	,,	airforce blue	
8 rows	,,	purple	
1 row	,,	airforce blue	
8 rows	,,	earth tweed	
1 row	,,	airforce blue	
8 rows	,,	purple	
1 row	,,	airforce blue	
8 rows	,,	airforce blue tweed	
1 row	,,	airforce blue	
8 rows	,,	black chenille	
1 row	,,	airforce blue	
9 rows	Fair Isle	airforce blue	navy
9 rows	,,	airforce blue	brown
1 row	slip	airforce blue	
8 rows	,,	black tweed	
1 row	,,	airforce blue	
8 rows	,,	rust	
1 row	,,	airforce blue	
8 rows	,,	black**	

The last 164 rows from ** to ** form the patt and are repeated throughout.

BACK
Bring forward 190 (190, 196, 196) needles on main bed to WP.
Using airforce blue cast on for side edge, using the closed edge method.
MT. Knit 2 (1, 2, 1) rows.
Insert punchcard and lock on correct row number for size being worked.
Set patt int memory.
RC 000.
Release card and work in pat sequence as given in chart to RC 99 (126, 135, 144).
Carriage at left.

Shape neck
Dec 1 st at left on next and every foll 9th row 4 times altogether.
Cont in patt to RC 210 (237, 246, 255).
Inc 1 st at left on next and every foll 9th row 4 times altogether.
Cont in patt to RC 338 (392, 410, 428).
Using airforce blue, knit 2 (1, 2, 1) rows.
Cast off (bind off).

FRONT
Work as given for back until RC 99 (126, 135, 144).
Carriage at left.

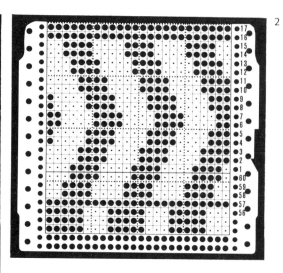

Shape neck.
Cast off (bind off) 5 sts at beg of next row.
Keeping patt correct, dec 1 st at neck edge on every row to RC 169 (196, 205, 214).
Inc 1 st at neck edge on every row until there are 185 (185, 191, 191) sts. Cast on 5 sts at beg of next row.
Keeping patt correct, knit to RC 338 (393, 410, 428).
Using airforce blue, knit 2 (1, 2, 1) rows.
Cast off (bind off).

SLEEVES
Beginning with the 66th needle to left of centre 0, bring forward 16 needles to WP.
Using airforce blue cast on for side edge of sleeve, using the closed edge method.
MT. Knit 2 rows.
Insert punchcard and lock on row 1.
Set patt into memory. RC 000.
Release card and working in patt sequence as given in chart, inc 1 st at right on every row until there are 132 sts. RC 116.
Work straight to RC 276.
Dec 1 st at right on every row until 16 sts rem. RC 392.
Using airforce blue, knit 2 rows.
Cast off (bind off).

PATTERN SEQUENCE FOR SLEEVES

ROWS	PATTERN SETTING	COLOUR IN FEEDER A	COLOUR IN FEEDER B
Join punchcards 1 and 2 together, then join into a circle to form 82 rows of patt beginning at row 1 on punchcard 1. Set to row 1 of patt			
1 row	slip	airforce blue	
8 rows	''	black tweed	
1 row	''	airforce blue	
8 rows	''	rust	
1 row	''	airforce blue	
8 rows	''	black	
1 row	''	airforce blue	
8 rows	''	mole chenille	
1 row	''	airforce blue	
8 rows	''	black	
1 row	''	airforce blue	
8 rows	''	rust	
1 row	''	airforce blue	
8 rows	''	black tweed	
1 row	''	airforce blue	
9 rows	Fair Isle	airforce blue	brown

ROWS	PATTERN SETTING	COLOUR IN FEEDER A	COLOUR IN FEEDER B
9 rows	''	airforce blue	navy
1 row	slip	airforce blue	
8 rows	''	black chenille	
1 row	''	airforce blue	
8 rows	''	airforce blue tweed	
1 row	''	airforce blue	
8 rows	''	purple	
1 row	''	airforce blue	
8 rows	''	earth tweed	
1 row	''	airforce blue	
8 rows	''	purple	
1 row	''	airforce blue	
8 rows	''	airforce blue tweed	
1 row	''	airforce blue	
8 rows	''	black chenille	
1 row	''	airforce blue	
9 rows	Fair Isle	airforce blue	navy
9 rows	''	airforce blue	brown

The last 164 rows form the pattern and are repeated throughout.

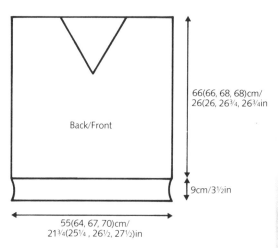

66(66, 68, 68)cm/
26(26, 26¾, 26¾in

Back/Front

9cm/3½in

55(64, 67, 70)cm/
21¾(25¼ , 26½, 27½)in

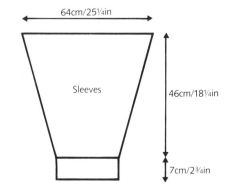

64cm/25¼in

Sleeves

46cm/18¼in

7cm/2¾in

NECKBAND
Join shoulder seams.
Bring forward 200 needles on each bed to WP.
Pushing back every 3rd needle to NWP, arrange needles
for 2 × 2 rib.
Using airforce blue cast on, ending with carriage at right.
RC 000. MT-3. Knit in stripes of 2 rows navy, 2 rows
airforce blue, 2 rows rust, 2 rows airforce blue, 2 rows
purple and 2 rows airforce blue until RC 28.
Transfer all sts to main bed. (Some needles will now have
2 sts on them.)
With WS of back and front facing, pick up 100 sts
between centre front neck and centre back neck and
place on to first 100 needles. Using airforce blue, cast off
(bind off) first 100 sts. Now pick up 100 sts along
remainder of back neck and second side of front neck
and place on to rem 100 needles. Using airforce blue,
cast off (bind off) rem sts.

WELTS
Bring forward 179 (183, 187, 191) needles on each bed
to WP. Pushing back every 3rd needle to NWP, arrange
needles for 2 × 2 rib.
Using airforce blue cast on, ending with carriage at right.
RC 000. MT–3. Knit in stripes of 2 rows navy, 2 rows,
airforce blue, 2 rows rust, 2 rows airforce blue, 2 rows
purple, 2 rows airforce blue until RC 47. Carriage at left.
Transfer all sts to main bed.
With WS of back facing, pick up 179 (183, 187, 191) sts
along lower edge and placed on to needles holding welt
sts.
MT + 1. Knit 1 row.
Cast off (bind off) loosely.

CUFFS
Bring forward 87 needles on each bed to WP. Pushing
back every 3rd needle to NWP, arrange needles for
2 × 2 rib.
Using airforce blue cast on, ending with carriage at right.
RC 000. MT–3. Knit in stripes of 2 rows navy, 2 rows,
airforce blue, 2 rows rust, 2 rows airforce blue, 2 rows
purple, 2 rows airforce blue until RC 35. Carriage at left.

Transfer all sts to main bed.
With WS of sleeve facing, pick up 87 sts along lower
edge of sleeve and place on to needles holding cuff sts.
MT + 1. Knit 1 row.
Cast off (bind off) loosely.

TO MAKE UP
Fold sleeves in half lengthwise, then placing folds to
shoulder seems, sew into position. Join side and sleeve
seams. Join neckband seam at centre front to form a
mitre, then slipstitch back remainder of seam to inside
centre front neckband.

*Above: The combination of
slip stitches and stripes
form the cable-textured
vertical bands on this stylish
sweater by Alison Taylor.*

RACHAEL GRIMMER

EASTERN INFLUENCE

Right: The back and fronts of this jacket are knitted sideways, using only a single bed machine.

MATERIALS
Rowan Light Tweed
300g/11oz charcoal (shade 210)
75g/3oz pebble (shade 203)
Rowan Fine Fleck Tweed
100g/4oz pink tweed (shade 410)
75g/3oz silver (shade 64)
25g/1oz dark pink (shade 412)
Rowan Botany 4 ply
150g/6oz fawn brown (shade 616)
50g/2oz cream (shade 83)
25g/1oz grey (shade 61)
50g/2oz pink (shade 69)
Rowan Fine Cotton Chenille
100g/4oz shark (shade 378)
50g/2oz carnation (shade 389)
6 large buttons

MEASUREMENTS
To fit bust 91–107cm/36–42in
Actual size
Bust 175cm/70in
Length 67cm/26½in
Sleeve seam 55cm/22in

TENSION
27 sts and 36 rows to 10cm/4in worked over st st with TD at approx 9

MACHINE
Any Brother standard gauge electronic or punchard machine or equivalent

BACK
Bring foward 115 needles at left of bed.
Cast on with waste yarn and knit 6 rows.
Cont in patt sequence from chart, shaping as given.

ROWS	PATTERN SETTING	COLOUR IN FEEDER A	COLOUR IN FEEDER B
Insert punchcards 1, 2, 3, 4, 5, 6, and 7 (joined together)			
Lock on row 1.			
1	plain	charcoal tweed	
Release card			
4	Fair Isle	charcoal tweed	bran tweed
15	''	charcoal tweed	pink tweed
12	''	charcoal tweed	brown
Using charcoal, cast on by hand 70 sts at right.			
Push 115 needles at left into HP.			
On rem needles work as follows:			
14	plain	charcoal tweed	
12	Fair Isle	charcoal tweed	brown
Make hem by picking up loops of first of 14 rows charcoal and place on to needles.			
Cast off (bind off) 10 sts at right, then bring all needles back into WP, 175 sts.			
2	plain	cream	
8	Fair Isle	silver tweed	shark
2	plain	shark	
2	''	dark pink	
2	''	grey	
10	Fair Isle	bran tweed	dark pink
2	plain	brown	
2	''	silver tweed	
2	''	shark	
2	''	charcoal tweed	
2	''	cream	
2	''	bran tweed	
6	Fair Isle	brown	pink tweed
2	plain	silver tweed	
2	''	shark	
2	''	charcoal tweed	
2	''	cream	
4	Fair Isle	dark pink tweed	carnation
2	plain	silver tweed	
2	''	charcoal tweed	
6	Fair Isle	dark pink	bran tweed
2	plain	brown	
2	''	charcoal tweed	
14	Fair Isle	pink tweed	shark
2	plain	brown	
2	''	cream	
2	''	bran tweed	
2	''	dark pink	
2	''	dark pink tweed	
2	''	shark	
2	''	silver tweed	
12	Fair Isle	charcoal tweed	brown
15	''	charcoal tweed	pink tweed
4	''	charcoal tweed	bran tweed
This is centre back, cont as follows:			
4	''	charcoal tweed	bran tweed
15	''	charcoal tweed	pink tweed
12	Fair Isle	charcoal tweed	brown
2	plain	silver tweed	
2	''	shark	
2	''	dark pink tweed	
2	''	dark pink	
2	plain	bran tweed	
2	''	cream	
2	plain	brown	
14	Fair Isle	light pink	shark
2	plain	charcoal tweed	
2	''	brown	
6	Fair Isle	dark pink	bran tweed
2	plain	charcoal tweed	
2	plain	silver tweed	
4	Fair Isle	dark pink tweed	carnation
2	plain	cream	
2	''	charcoal tweed	
2	''	shark	
2	plain	silver tweed	
6	Fair Isle	brown	pink tweed
2	plain	bran tweed	
2	''	cream	
2	''	charcoal tweed	
2	''	shark	
2	''	silver tweed	
2	plain	brown	
10	Fair Isle	bran tweed	dark pink
2	plain	grey	
2	''	dark pink	

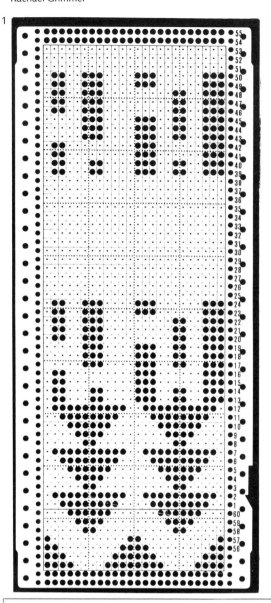

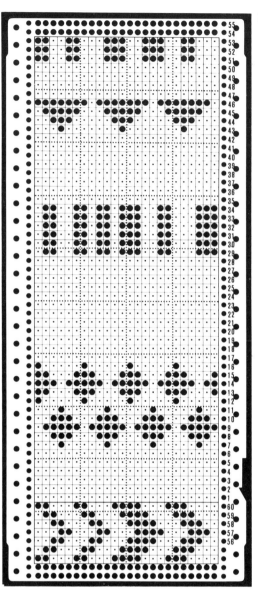

ROWS	PATTERN SETTING	COLOUR IN FEEDER A	COLOUR IN FEEDER B
2	plain	shark	
8	Fair Isle	silver tweed	shark
1	plain	cream	

Lock card and knit 1 row plain cream.
Cast on 10 sts at right, then push 115 needles at left into HP.
Cont on rem sts at follows: Release card.

ROWS	PATTERN SETTING	COLOUR IN FEEDER A	COLOUR IN FEEDER B
12	Fair Isle	charcoal tweed	brown
14	plain	charcoal tweed	

Make hem by picking up loops from first of last 26 rows and place on to needles.

Using charcoal, cast off (bind off) by hand 70 sts at right.
Push rem 115 needles at left into WP.
Work as follows:

ROWS	PATTERN SETTING	COLOUR IN FEEDER A	COLOUR IN FEEDER B
12	Fair Isle	charcoal tweed	brown
15	,,	charcoal tweed	pink tweed
4	Fair Isle	charcoal tweed	bran tweed
1	plain	charcoal tweed	

Using waste yarn, knit 6 rows.
Release sts from machine.

RIGHT FRONT
Bring forward 115 needles at left of bed.
Cast on with waste yarn and knit 6 rows.
Cont in patt sequence from chart, shaping as given.

109

Left: The sleeves are gathered on to a Fair Isle cuff by placing two stitches on to each needle.

ROWS	PATTERN SETTING	COLOUR IN FEEDER A	COLOUR IN FEEDER B
Insert punchcards 1, 2, 3, 4, 5, 6 and 7 (joined together)			
Lock on row 1.			
1	plain	charcoal tweed	
Release card			
4	Fair Isle	charcoal tweed	bran tweed
15	,,	charcoal tweed	pink tweed
12	,,	charcoal tweed	brown

Using charcoal, cast on by hand 70 sts at right.
Push 115 needles at left into HP.
On rem needles work as follows:

ROWS	PATTERN SETTING	COLOUR IN FEEDER A	COLOUR IN FEEDER B
14	plain	charcoal tweed	
12	Fair Isle	charcoal tweed	brown

Make hem by picking up loops of first of 14 rows charcoal and place on to needles.
Cast off (bind off) 10 sts at right, then bring all needles back into WP. 175 sts.

ROWS	PATTERN SETTING	COLOUR IN FEEDER A	COLOUR IN FEEDER B
2	plain	cream	
8	Fair Isle	silver tweed	shark
2	plain	shark	
2	,,	dark pink	
2	,,	grey	
10	Fair Isle	bran tweed	dark pink
2	plain	brown	
2	,,	silver tweed	
2	,,	shark	
2	,,	charcoal tweed	
2	,,	cream	

Note RC reading. Lock card.
Make pocket
Push 24 needles at left and 124 needles at right into HP.
Work on rem 27 sts in WP as follows:
Set machine for plain knitting.
MT−1. Knit 70 rows charcoal tweed, then 8 rows bran tweed.

Return all needles to WP. Release card.
Reset RC to row noted.
Cont across all sts as follows:

ROWS	PATTERN SETTING	COLOUR IN FEEDER A	COLOUR IN FEEDER B
2	,,	bran tweed	
4	Fair Isle	brown	pink tweed

Make hem over pocket by picking up loops of first row in bran tweed and place on to needles.

ROWS	PATTERN SETTING	COLOUR IN FEEDER A	COLOUR IN FEEDER B
2	Fair Isle	brown	pink tweed
2	plain	silver tweed	
2	,,	shark	
2	,,	charcoal tweed	
2	,,	cream	
4	Fair Isle	dark pink tweed	carnation
2	plain	silver tweed	
2	,,	charcoal tweed	
6	Fair Isle	dark pink	bran tweed
2	plain	brown	
2	,,	charcoal tweed	
14	Fair Isle	pink tweed	shark
2	plain	brown	
2	,,	cream	
2	plain	bran tweed	
2	,,	dark pink	
2	,,	dark pink tweed	
2	,,	shark	
2	,,	silver tweed	

Cast off (bind off) 15 sts at right for neck.

ROWS	PATTERN SETTING	COLOUR IN FEEDER A	COLOUR IN FEEDER B
12	Fair Isle	charcoal tweed	brown
15	,,	charcoal tweed	pink tweed
4	,,	charcoal tweed	bran tweed

Using waste yarn, knit 6 rows.
Release sts from machine.

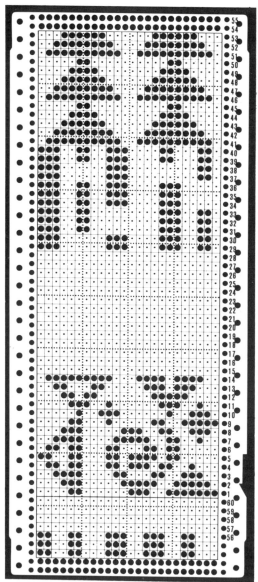

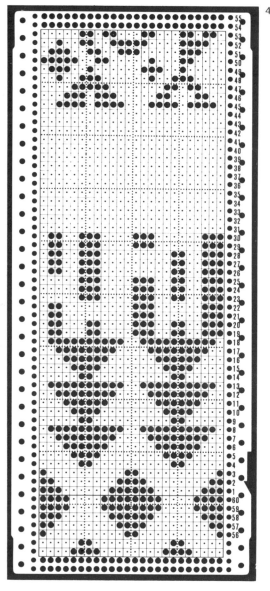

LEFT FRONT

Work as given for right front, reversing all shaping and pocket placing by reading right for left and left for right.

SLEEVES

Bring forward 140 needles to WP.
Cast on by hand with charcoal tweed.
Cont in patt sequence from chart.

ROWS	PATTERN SETTING	COLOUR IN FEEDER A	COLOUR IN FEEDER B
Insert punchcards 8, 9, 10, 11 and 12 (joined together)			
Lock on row 1.			
2	plain	charcoal tweed	
Release card			
12	Fair Isle	charcoal tweed	brown
15	''	charcoal tweed	pink tweed
4	''	charcoal tweed	bran tweed
4	''	charcoal tweed	silver
15	''	charcoal tweed	carnation
12	''	charcoal tweed	brown
2	plain	cream	
7	Fair Isle	silver tweed	shark

ROWS	PATTERN SETTING	COLOUR IN FEEDER A	COLOUR IN FEEDER B
2	plain	shark	
2	''	dark pink tweed	
2	''	grey	
10	Fair Isle	bran tweed	dark pink
2	plain	brown	
2	''	silver tweed	
2	''	shark	
2	''	charcoal tweed	
2	''	cream	
2	''	bran tweed	
6	Fair Isle	brown	pink tweed
2	plain	silver tweed	
2	''	shark	
2	''	charcoal tweed	
2	''	cream	
4	Fair Isle	dark pink tweed	carnation
2	plain	silver tweed	
2	''	grey	
6	Fair Isle	bran tweed	dark pink
2	plain	brown	
2	''	charcoal tweed	
14	Fair Isle	pink tweed	shark
2	plain	brown	
2	''	cream	

5

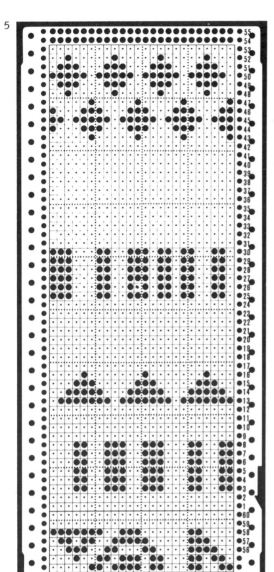

6

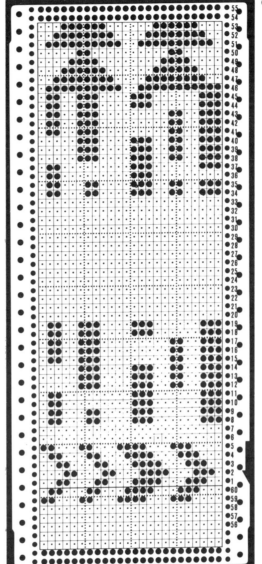

7

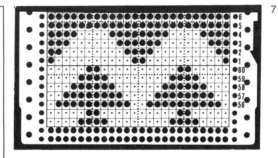

ROWS	PATTERN SETTING	COLOUR IN FEEDER A	COLOUR IN FEEDER B
2	plain	bran tweed	
2	,,	dark pink	
2	,,	dark pink tweed	
2	,,	shark	
2	,,	silver tweed	
12	Fair Isle	charcoal tweed	brown
15	,,	charcoal tweed	carnation
4	,,	charcoal tweed	silver tweed
2	plain	dark pink	

Using waste yarn, knit 6 rows.
Release sts from machine.

CUFFS
Bring forward 70 needles to WP.
Placing 2 sts on to each needle, pick up sts from last row worked in dark pink on sleeves and hook on to needles.
Insert punchcard 13 and lock on row 1.
RC 000, MT−1. Cont in patt from chart.

ROWS	PATTERN SETTING	COLOUR IN FEEDER A	COLOUR IN FEEDER B
1	plain	charcoal tweed	
Release card			
24	Fair Isle	charcoal tweed	brown
28	plain	charcoal tweed	

Make hem by picking up loops from first row and placing on to needles.
MT + 1, knit 1 row charcoal tweed.
Cast off (bind off).

Rachael Grimmer

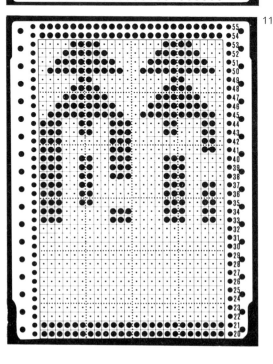

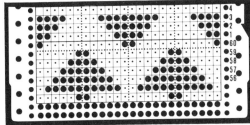

method.
Work as given for neckband from * to *.

JOINS SIDE SEAMS AND ATTACH WELT
Bring forward 115 needles to WP.
With WS of back facing, pick up 115 sts held on waste yard at side seam and place on to needles.
With RS of front facing, pick up corresponding sts and place on to same needles.
MT + 1, Knit 1 row in charcoal tweed.
Cast off (bind off).
Rep with second side seam.
Join centre back welt seam.
Forming an inverted pleat of approx 10cm/4in each side of side seams and with right sides together, backstitch welt into place along lower edge.

BUTTON BORDER
Bring forward 175 needles to WP.
With WS of left front facing, pick up 175 sts evenly along left front edge.
Work as given for neckband from * to *.

BUTTONHOLE BORDER
Work as given for button border, working buttonholes on rows 8 and 23 as follows:
Buttonhole row
Miss first 6 sts at left, * using a spare length of yarn, cast off (bind off) the next 6 sts, then cast them on again using the same length of yarn *, miss the next 26 sts, [rep from * to *, miss the next 25 sts] 3 times, rep from * to *, miss the next 26 sts, rep from * to *, then miss the last 6 sts.
Cont knitting in patt to next buttonhole row.

TO MAKE UP
Neatly oversew top and bottom edges of button and buttonhole borders. Sew on buttons. Join row ends of pocket linings. Sew in sleeves, joining row ends at top of sleeves to cast on/off sts at armholes.
Join sleeve seams. Make 3 pleats along shoulder edge and stich securely on inside to hold.

SHOULDER STRAPS
Bring forward 60 needles to WP.
Insert punchcard 11 and lock on row 11.
Using charcoal tweed, cast on using the closed edge method.
MT−1, RC 000. cont from chart as follows:

ROWS	PATTERN SETTING	COLOUR IN FEEDER A	COLOUR IN FEEDER B
1	plain	charcoal tweed	
Release card			
12	Fair Isle	charcoal tweed	brown
1	plain	charcoal tweed	
Cast off (bind off).			

NECKBAND
Sew each shoulder strip along each front shoulder edge, then join to corresponding rows on back.
Tuck in excess on shoulder hem and neatly join seam at top of shoulder.
Bring forward 140 needles.
With WS facing, pick up 140 sts evenly round neck and place on to needles.
* Insert punchcard 11 and lock on row 11.
RC 000, MT−1. Knit 9 rows charcoal tweed.
Set machine for Fair Isle. Release card.
With charcoal tweed in feeder A and brown in feeder B, knit 6 rows.
Set machine for plain knitting.
With charcoal tweed, knit to RC 30.
Make hem by picking up loops of first row in charcoal tweed and placing on to needles.
MT + 1. Knit 1 row.
Cast off (bind off). *

WELT (make 2 pieces)
Bring forward 160 needles to WP.
Using charcoal tweed, cast on using closed edge

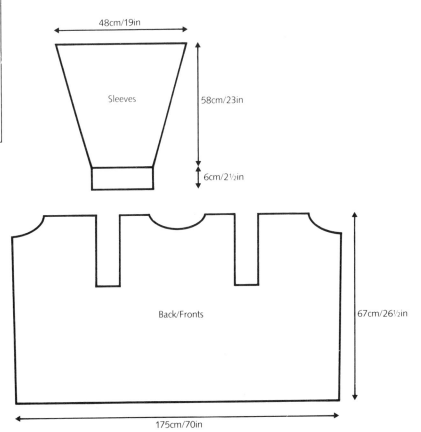

Rachael Grimmer

TRIBAL COAT

Right: The mixture of browns and neutral shades blend together to form a very attractive pattern on this luxurious coat.

MATERIALS
Rowan Botany 4 ply
400g/14oz black (shade 62)
25g/1oz white (shade 1)
100g/4oz tan (shade 87)
Rowan Lightweight Tweed
100g/4oz autumn (shade 205)
100g/4oz pebble (shade 203)
200g/8oz earth (shade 206)
200g/8oz ebony (shade 207)
200g/8oz charcoal (shade 210)
Rowan Fine Fleck Tweed
50g/2oz silver (shade 64)
Rowan Fine Cotton Chenille
100g/4oz ecru (shade 376)
100g/4oz bran (shade 381)
7 buttons and 1 press fastener

MEASUREMENTS
To fit bust 91–107cm/36–42in
Actual size
Bust 220cm/87in
Length 77cm/30½in
Sleeve length 54cm/21½in

TENSION
26 sts and 40 rows to 10cm/4in worked over Fair Isle
with TD at approx 9

MACHINE
Any Brother standard gauge electronic or punchcard
machine or equivalent.

BACK AND FRONTS
Using black, cast on 200 sts for centre front edge.
Setting machine as given in chart, work as follows:

ROWS	PATTERN SETTING	COLOUR IN FEEDER A	COLOUR IN FEEDER B	RC
Insert punchcard 5				
Locked on row 1				
MT–3. RC 000.				
14	plain	black		14
Buttonhole row				

Miss first 6 sts at left, * using a spare length of yarn, cast off (bind off) the next 6 sts, then cast them on again using the same length of yarn *, miss the next 31 sts, [rep from * to *, miss the next 30 sts] 3 times, rep from * to *, miss the next 31 sts, rep from * to *, then miss the last 6 sts.
Cont knitting in patt to next buttonhole row.

ROWS	PATTERN SETTING	COLOUR IN FEEDER A	COLOUR IN FEEDER B	RC
20	plain	black		34
1	,,	earth		35
2	,,	ebony		37
1	,,	earth		38
Release card				
2	Fair Isle	charcoal	autumn tweed	40
2	,,	charcoal	pebble	42
2	,,	charcoal	silver	44
2	,,	charcoal	white chenille	46

ROWS	PATTERN SETTING	COLOUR IN FEEDER A	COLOUR IN FEEDER B	RC
Buttonhole row				

Miss first 6 sts at left, * using a spare length of yarn, cast off (bind off) the next 6 sts, then cast them on again using the same length of yarn *, miss the next 31 sts, [rep from * to *, miss the next 30 sts] 3 times, rep from * to *, miss the next 31 sts, rep from * to *, then miss the last 6 sts.

ROWS	PATTERN SETTING	COLOUR IN FEEDER A	COLOUR IN FEEDER B	RC
2	plain	charcoal		48
2	Fair Isle	charcoal	bran chenille	50
2	,,	charcoal	tan	52
2	,,	charcoal	earth tweed	54
2	,,	charcoal	ebony tweed	56
3	plain	black		59

Make hem by picking up loops of first row in black and placing on to needles. (For left front omit buttonholes and work last 59 rows in reverse, making hem on last row.)
Cast off 15 sts at left for buttonhole border.
(Cast on 15 sts at left for button border on return rows.)
Insert punchcards 1, 2, 3 and 4 (joined together).

ROWS	PATTERN COLOUR IN SETTING	COLOUR IN FEEDER A	COLOUR IN FEEDER B	
Set patt into memory. MT. Reset RC to 000.				
2	Fair Isle	charcoal	white chenille	2
3	''	earth tweed	bran chenille	5
4	''	charcoal	tan	9
5	''	ebony tweed	pebble	14
6	''	black	autumn tweed	20

Cast on 15 sts at left for right front neck shaping.)
(Cast off 15 sts at left for left front neck shaping.)

2	plain	earth tweed		22
2	Fair Isle	charcoal	autumn tweed	24
2	''	charcoal	pebble	26
2	''	charcoal	silver	28
2	''	charcoal	white chenille	30
2	plain	charcoal		32
2	Fair Isle	charcoal	bran chenille	34
2	''	charcoal	tan	36
2	''	charcoal	earth tweed	38
2	''	charcoal	ebony tweed	40
2	plain	autumn tweed		42
2	Fair Isle	ebony tweed	black	44
2	''	ebony tweed	charcoal	46
2	''	ebony tweed	silver	48
2	''	ebony tweed	white	50
2	''	ebony tweed	white chenille	52
2	''	ebony tweed	pebble	54
2	''	ebony tweed	autumn tweed	56
2	''	ebony tweed	bran tweed	58
2	''	ebony tweed	tan	60
2	''	ebony tweed	earth tweed	62
2	''	ebony tweed	black	64
2	''	ebony tweed	charcoal	66
2	''	ebony tweed	silver	68
2	''	ebony tweed	white	70
2	''	ebony tweed	pebble	72
2	''	ebony tweed	autumn tweed	74
2	''	ebony tweed	earth tweed	76
2	''	ebony tweed	tan	78
2	''	ebony tweed	autumn tweed	80
2	''	ebony tweed	bran chenille	82
2	plain	pebble		84
2	''	autumn tweed		86
2	''	earth tweed		88
2	''	ebony tweed		90

Note RC reading. Lock punchcard.
Make pocket.
Push 50 needles at right and 120 needles at left into HP.
Work on rem 30 sts in WP as follows:
Set machine for plain knitting.
MT−1. Knit 8 rows earth tweed, then 70 rows black.
Return all needles to WP.
Reset RC to row noted. Release punchcard.
Cont across all sts as follows:

2	Fair Isle	earth tweed	black	92
2	''	earth tweed	charcoal	94
2	''	earth tweed	silver	96
2	''	earth tweed	white	98
2	plain	earth tweed		100
2	Fair Isle	earth tweed	pebble	102
2	''	earth tweed	bran chenille	104
2	''	earth tweed	autumn	106
2	''	earth tweed	tan	108
2	plain	white		110
2	''	ebony		112
2	''	silver		114

ROWS	PATTERN COLOUR IN SETTING	COLOUR IN FEEDER A	COLOUR IN FEEDER B	
2	''	ebony		116
2	''	autumn		118
2	''	ebony		120
2	''	pebble		122
2	''	ebony		124
2	''	tan		126
2	''	black		128
6	Fair Isle	charcoal	white chenille	134
2	plain	black		136
6	Fair Isle	ebony	bran chenille	142
2	plain	silver		144
2	''	earth		146
2	''	charcoal		148
2	''	earth		150
2	''	bran		152
2	''	earth		154
2	''	pebble		156
2	''	earth		158
2	''	autumn		160
2	''	earth		162
2	Fair Isle	black	ebony	164
2	''	black	earth	166
2	''	black	charcoal	168

2
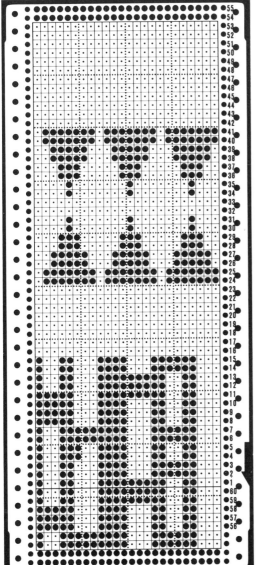

3
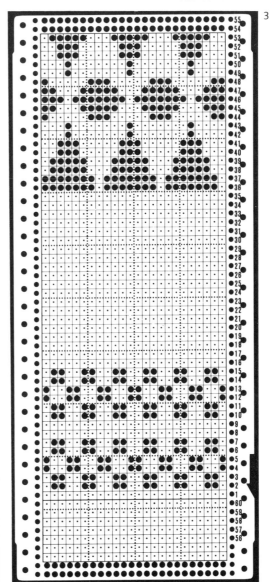

4
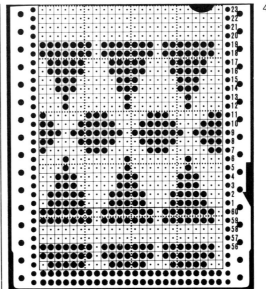

ROWS	PATTERN SETTING	COLOUR IN FEEDER A	COLOUR IN FEEDER B	
2	,,	black	silver	170
5	,,	black	white chenille	175
2	,,	black	silver	177
2	,,	black	charcoal	179
2	,,	black	earth	181
2	,,	black	ebony	183
1	plain	black		184

Cast off 60 sts at left for armhole, when knitting in reverse back through chart, cast on 60 sts.

1	plain	black		185
2	Fair Isle	black	ebony	187
2	,,	black	earth	189
2	,,	black	tan	191
2	,,	black	pebble	193
5	,,	black	white chenille	198
2	,,	black	pebble	200
2	,,	black	tan	202
2	,,	black	earth	204
2	,,	black	ebony	206
2	plain	black		208

The last 2 rows form the right side seam.
Take out pattern cards and inserting them back into the machine in reverse order (upside down), work in pattern from chart, starting at row 206 and working backwards to row 1, shaping for armholes where indicated but not shaping neck across back. RC 414.
Now work all 414 rows once more, then working in reverse order, work button border as given for buttonhole border, omitting the buttonholes.

SHOULDER STRIPS
Bring forward 60 needles to WP.
Insert punchcard 5 and lock on row 1.
Using charcoal tweed, cast on using the closed edge method.
MT−3. RC 000. Cont from chart as follows:

ROWS	PATTERN SETTING	COLOUR IN FEEDER A	COLOUR IN FEEDER B
4	plain	black	
Release card			
2	Fair Isle	charcoal	ebony
2	''	charcoal	earth
2	''	charcoal	tan
2	''	charcoal	bran chenille
2	plain	charcoal	
2	Fair Isle	charcoal	white chenille
2	''	charcoal	silver
2	''	charcoal	pebble
2	''	charcoal	autumn
1	plain	earth	
2	''	ebony	
1	''	earth	
2	Fair Isle	charcoal	autumn
2	''	charcoal	pebble
2	''	charcoal	silver
2	''	charcoal	white chenille
2	plain	charcoal	
2	Fair Isle	charcoal	bran chenille
2	''	charcoal	tan
2	''	charcoal	earth
2	''	charcoal	ebony
4	plain	black	
Cast off.			

NECKBAND
Sew each shoulder strip along each front shoulder edge, then join to corresponding rows on back.
Bring forward 130 needles.
With WS facing, pick up 130 sts evenly round neck and place on to needles.
Insert punchcard 5 and lock on row 1.
RC 000. MT−3.

ROWS	PATTERN SETTING	COLOUR IN FEEDER A	COLOUR IN FEEDER B
4	plain	black	
2	Fair Isle	charcoal	ebony
2	''	charcoal	earth
2	''	charcoal	tan
2	''	charcoal	bran chenille
2	plain	charcoal	
2	Fair Isle	charcoal	white chenille
2	''	charcoal	silver

ROWS	PATTERN SETTING	COLOUR IN FEEDER A	COLOUR IN FEEDER B
2	''	charcoal	pebble
2	''	charcoal	autumn
2	plain	earth	
2	''	ebony	
35	''	black	

Make hem by picking up loops of first row in black and placing on to needles.
MT + 1. Knit 1 row.
Cast off (bind off).

SLEEVES
Bring forward 150 needles to WP.
With black, cast on using the closed edge method.
Insert card 6 and lock on row 4 of patt.
MT. RC 000. Cont in patt from chart as follows:

ROWS	PATTERN SETTING	COLOUR IN FEEDER A	COLOUR IN FEEDER B
4	plain	black	
Release card			
2	Fair Isle	black	ebony tweed
2	''	black	earth tweed
2	''	black	tan
Decreasing 1 st each end of next and every foll 10th row until 120 sts rem, cont as follows:			
2	Fair Isle	black	pebble
5	''	black	white chenille
2	''	black	pebble
2	''	black	tan
2	''	black	earth tweed
2	''	black	ebony tweed
Insert punchcard 5 (joined into a circle)			
Lock on row 1			
3	plain	black	
Release card			
2	Fair Isle	black	white chenille
2	''	black	white
2	''	black	silver
2	''	black	charcoal
1	plain	black	
1	''	charcoal	
2	Fair Isle	charcoal	black
2	''	charcoal	ebony tweed
2	''	charcoal	earth tweed
2	''	charcoal	autumn tweed
2	plain	tan	
2	''	bran chenille	
2	Fair Isle	earth tweed	black
2	''	earth tweed	charcoal
2	''	earth tweed	silver
2	''	earth tweed	white
2	plain	earth tweed	
2	Fair Isle	earth tweed	pebble
2	''	earth tweed	bran chenille
2	''	earth tweed	tan
2	''	earth tweed	autumn tweed
2	plain	ebony tweed	
2	''	black	
2	Fair Isle	charcoal	ebony tweed
2	''	charcoal	earth tweed
2	''	charcoal	tan
2	''	charcoal	bran chenille
2	plain	charcoal	

ROWS	PATTERN SETTING	COLOUR IN FEEDER A	COLOUR IN FEEDER B
2	Fair Isle	charcoal	white chenille
2	''	charcoal	silver
2	''	charcoal	pebble
2	''	charcoal	autumn tweed
4	plain	earth tweed	
2	Fair Isle	charcoal	autumn tweed
2	''	charcoal	pebble
2	''	charcoal	silver
2	''	charcoal	white chenille
2	plain	charcoal	
2	Fair Isle	charcoal	bran chenille
2	''	charcoal	tan
2	''	charcoal	earth tweed
2	''	charcoal	ebony tweed
4	plain	black	
2	Fair Isle	earth tweed	ebony tweed
2	''	earth tweed	charcoal
2	''	earth tweed	tan
2	''	earth tweed	bran chenille
2	plain	earth tweed	
2	Fair Isle	earth tweed	pebble
2	''	earth tweed	white
2	''	earth tweed	silver
2	''	earth tweed	charcoal
4	plain	black	
2	Fair Isle	ebony tweed	earth tweed
2	''	ebony tweed	tan
2	''	ebony tweed	autumn tweed
2	''	ebony tweed	bran chenille
2	plain	ebony tweed	
2	Fair Isle	ebony tweed	pebble
2	''	ebony tweed	white
2	''	ebony tweed	silver
2	''	ebony tweed	charcoal
4	plain	black	

Using waste yarn, knit 6 rows. Release sts from machine.

WELT (make 2 pieces)
Bring forward 160 needles to WP.
Using black, cast on using closed edge method.
Work 48 rows as given for shoulder strips, then knit 48 rows black.
Make hem by picking up sts of first row and placing on to needles. MT + 1. Knit 1 row. Cast off (bind off) loosely.
Join centre back welt seam.
Gathering lower edge of coat to fit, backstitch welt into place along lower edge.

CUFFS
Bring forward 70 needles to WP. Placing 2 sts on to each needle, pick up sts from last row worked in black on sleeves and hook on to needles.
Insert punchcard 5 and lock on row 1. RC 000. MT−1.
Complete as given for neckband.

TO MAKE UP
Neatly oversew top and bottom edges of button and buttonhole borders. Sew on buttons. Join row ends of pocket linings. Sew in sleeves, joining row ends at top of sleeves to cast on/off sts at armholes. Join sleeve seams. Sew on buttons. Sew button to right welt, then sew on press fastener under button on right welt and to corresponding edge of left welt.

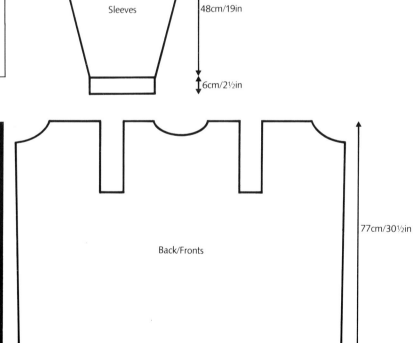

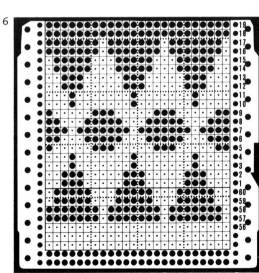

TECHNICAL DATA

BEFORE YOU START

Machines

On a knitting machine, the distance between the needles within the bed determines which thickness of yarn can be knitted on it: this is called the gauge. Fine-gauge machines are used for knitting fine industrial-type yarns, standard-gauge machines for knitting anything from 2 ply (fingering) to a fine double knitting (knitted worsted) weight, and chunky machines for the more usual hand-knitting and fancy yarns.

All the garments in this book have been knitted on standard-gauge machines, and each pattern states which type of machine is needed to produce a particular stitch pattern.

The simpler, plain and striped garments can be made on any basic model with the help of a ribbing attachment. These machines are usually bought by the beginner who wants a moderately priced machine to learn on. They are able to knit simple patterns by selecting the needles, either manually or by pressing buttons, on every row.

Next come the punchcard models, which can produce all-over repeating patterns or single motifs. The pattern is first punched, as holes, on to a plastic sheet and then fed into the machine.

These machines restrict you to a set number of stitches, generally 24, across the width of the pattern and the majority of garments in this book have been knitted using one of these machines.

Finally, in the higher price range, come the electronic machines. These are far more complicated to learn but have the advantage that patterns can be worked over any number of stitches up to 200 in width. The patterns for these machines are simply marked on to special sheets of paper, using the pen provided.

On most of the garments in this book the ribbed welts (ribbings), cuffs, collars and borders have been made by using a ribbing attachment, but, as this is quite an expensive optional extra, instructions are given in the technical hints section on how to work them on a single-bed machine.

Before following any of the patterns, check with your instruction manual whether the techniques given in the pattern are correct for your machine, if you are following a punchcard pattern, for example, some of the older punchcard machines have the background and second colours reversed so that the hole punched in the card represent the background colour.

If you are not sure which techniques are right for your machine, knit a small swatch of the stitch pattern first to see which settings you should use to achieve the desired result — this swatch can then be used to check your tension.

Yarn

Within each pattern yarns have been specified for using in making your garment. If you use the correct yarn and achieve the correct tension, you should be completely satisfied with the completed garment.

If you cannot easily obtain the correct yarn, you can substitute a yarn of similar thickness. To do this satisfactorily, check first on the approximate thickness of the yarn, the tension it knits to, and the composition.

If you are not sure, see if you can purchase a small amount of the yarn first in order to try it out and compare it with the look of the yarn in the picture. Check to see that it knits to the correct tension without looking so loose that the garment will not hold its shape or so tight that it will not hang correctly. Finally, remember that the quantities stated are approximate and that if you use a different yarn, the amount of the yarn you choose could vary quite considerably from that quoted.

Tension

All the measurements of each garment have been calculated according to the number of stitches and rows worked to a given tension. This means that if the pattern quotes 27 stitches and 39 rows to 10 cm (4 in) measured over stocking (stockinette) stitch with a tension-dial setting of approximately 7, it is vital that you achieve the tension of 27 stitches and 39 rows, although the tension-dial setting is not so important and could be as low as 5 or as high as 9 as long as it produces the correct tension.

When working a tension swatch, always cast on at least 10 more stitches and work at least 10 more rows than quoted in the tension specified to give an accurate reading.

Abbreviations

alt	alternate(ly)
beg	beginning
cm	entimetre(s)
cont	continu(e)(ing)
dec	decreas(e)(ing)
foll	following
g	grams
HP	holding position
in	inch(es)
inc	increas(e)(ing)
K	knit
mm	millimetres
MT	main tension
MT−1, MT−2, MT−3	one, two or three full sizes tighter than main tension
MT+1, MT+2, MT+3	one, two or three full sizes looser than main tension
NWP	non-working position
oz	ounces
P	purl
patt	pattern
RC	row counter
rem	remain(ing)
rep	repeat
st(s)	stitch(es)
st st	stocking stitch (stockinette stitch)
tog	together
WP	working position

TECHNICAL DATA

ADVICE FOR AMERICAN KNITTERS

Most of the terms in this book are the same in English and American terminology. The main differences are between metric and imperial measurements and weights. Where appropriate, the imperial measurements and weights have been given after the metric ones within every pattern.

The terms which vary are given with their equivalents below:

UK	US
cast off	bind off
slipstitch	tack down
stocking stitch	stockinette stitch
tension	gauge
4 ply	sport
double knitting	knitting worsted
Aran	fisherman
chunky	bulky
colourway(s)	choice of colour(s)

Floats

A few of the garments have larger colour patterns which leave long floats on the inside of the fabric. Although they have been kept to a minimum, these can be a nuisance, especially in the sleeves.

If you are afraid that these floats might catch and spoil the look of your garment, there are two methods of dealing with them. The first is to use iron-on interfacing fabric to cover the floats, although this can be a little bit tricky to put on properly. The second is to use thread matching the main yarn and catch (tack) down the floats to the inside of the garment at regular intervals.

Measurements

The measurements on the diagrams and patterns are given throughout in both centimetres and inches. The figures in brackets refer to the larger sizes; if only one figure is given, then this refers to all sizes.

Punchcards and charts

On the patterned garments in this book it is necessary to punch the designs on to a punchcard or mark up on to the special sheets for the electronic machines.

Most punchcard machines have the contrast colour as the one which is translated into the holes on the card, but check with your instruction manual to see if this is true of your machine. There is usually a minimum number of rows required in order that the punchcard can be formed into a circle and clipped together. Again check with your instruction book, and if the pattern repeat does not give enough rows, then just punch the pattern twice in order to give enough rows. Always take note, perhaps when working your tension sample, of the row number marked on the punchcard that signals that the first row of pattern is to be knitted. Different machines need a different number of rows for the card to be wound into the machine before the punched holes are read, and if the correct make of punchcard is not easily available for your machine, then the card you use may not necessarily show row 1 when the first row of pattern is about to be knitted.

Electronic machines differ from punchcard machines in the way they set and read the pattern. They also give far more choice in that, at the flick of a switch, the pattern can be reversed, turned upside down or have the colours reversed.

You will see throughout this book that all the punchcards seem to be the wrong way round to the pattern on the garments. This is because you always work with the back of the work facing you. As soon as you turn the work the right way round, the patterns will look the same as in the pictures.

There can be no hard and fast rules for marking up a punchcard or pattern sheet, as new models are coming on to the market all the time, so if you have any questions, please follow the only rule that is always true: check with the instruction manual for your machine.

TECHNIQUES

Casting on

There are two main methods of casting on to a single bed in machine knitting. The first is the nylon-cord method, which is very quick and easy but leaves an unfinished edge and so is only suitable for tension swatches, stitch samples or casting on with waste yarn when making a hem. The second is the closed-edge method, which is a little slower, but gives a neat finished edge that resembles the hand-knit method of casting on.

Casting on with nylon cord

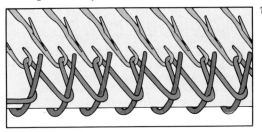

1. Bring forward the required number of needles to working position. Thread the carriage with the main yarn and set the tension slightly looser than the main tension for the yarn. Holding the end of the yarn from the cariage down below the needlebed, move the carriage from right to left over the needles so that the main yarn forms a zigzag between the hooks on the needles and the sinker posts.

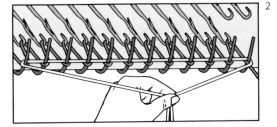

2. Take out the nylon cord, supplied with the machine, and lay it over the zigzag formed by the main yarn, making sure that it passes between the needle hooks and the sinker posts. Hold both ends of the nylon cord firmly with the left hand beneath the needlebed, pulling it tightly against the main yarn. Set the tension to main tension.

TECHNICAL DATA

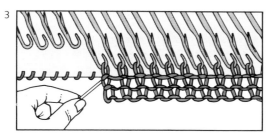

3. Set the machine to knit all the needles, and knit about six rows. Carefully pull out the nylon cord from one end, then continue to knit as required.

Casting on with a closed edge

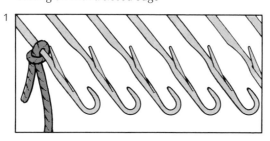

1. Bring forward the required number of needles to holding position. Set the machine to knit all the needles and the tension to main tension. Thread the carriage with the main yarn and make a slip loop near the end of the yarn. Place this loop over the needle furthest away from the carriage.

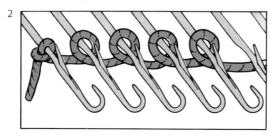

2. Holding the main yarn in your right hand, wind it anticlockwise round each needle, working from left to right. When winding the yarn, keep it fairly loose; otherwise, the loops formed on the needles will not knit properly when the carriage is passed over them. When the yarn has been wound round all the needles, pull back the yarn through the tension mast to take up any slackness, then knit the row. Continue knitting as required.

Casting off (Binding off)

The two most common methods of casting off are taking the fabric off on to waste yarn and the transfer-tool method. The first is quick and simple, ideal for tension swatches and stitch samples, or when stitches are to be picked up again at a later stage in making the garment. The second method is used when shaping at a neck or armhole, or if a closed, finished edge is required.

Casting off with waste yarn

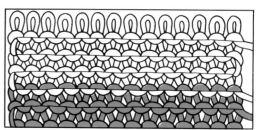

On completion of the required number of rows in main yarn, break off the yarn and unthread the carriage. Rethread the carriage with a contrasting yarn of similar thickness to the main yarn, and knit about six rows. Break off the contrast yarn and unthread the carriage. Remove any weights from the work. Then, supporting the fabric with your free hand, run the carriage once across the stitches, causing them to 'drop off' the needles. The waste yarn will hold the stitches in main yarn securely until required later.

Casting off (binding off) with a transfer tool

On completion of the required number of rows in the main yarn, end with carriage at the right-hand side of the needlebed.

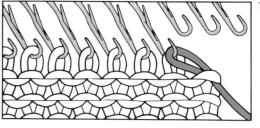

1. Using the single transfer tool, move the first stitch at the right-hand side on to the adjacent needle to the left, so that there are two stitches on this needle. Push the empty needle back into non-working position.

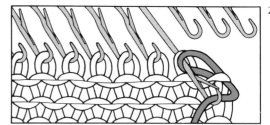

2. Push the needle holding two stitches forward so that both stiches lie behind the latch, leaving the latch in the open position. Take the yarn from the carriage in your left hand and lay it loosely across the hook, then close the latch over the yarn.

TECHNICAL DATA

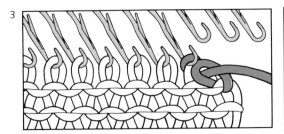

3. Holding the needle butt in your right hand, gently draw the loop of yarn in the needle hook through the two stitches behind the latch, then place the needle back into working position.

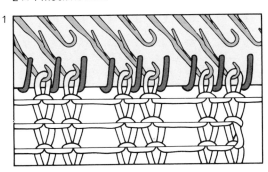

4. Repeat steps 1 to 3 until the required number of stitches have been cast off. If you are casting off all the stitches, break the yarn and thread it through last stitch, pulling up tightly to secure. In order to prevent the stitches being cast off too tightly, and to give an even finish, pass the yarn used for casting off in front of the sinker post between each cast-off stitch. This will have the effect of holding the knitting on the machine until the casting off is complete, when it can then be carefully lifted off.

Alternative Methods of ribbing

Most of the garments in this book have had the welts (ribbing), cuffs and borders knitted on a machine with a ribbing attachment. Alternatively, on a single bed machine the ribs can be worked as a mock rib hem, or hand knitted.

2 × 1 mock rib hem

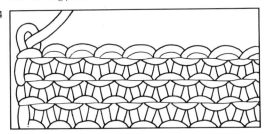

1. Bring forward to working position the required number of needles, as given in the pattern, for the piece of knitting after the rib has been knitted. Push every third needle back to non-working position. Cast on with waste yarn and work six rows, then change to main yarn and a tension approximately four numbers tighter than main tension and work enough rows to form twice the depth of the completed hem.

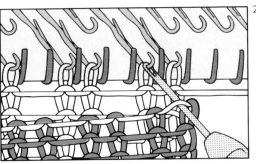

2. Fold the hem in half, allowing the waste yarn to roll forward. Using the single transfer tool, pick up the short loop between the first two stitches in the first row of main yarn and place it on to the second needle in working position.

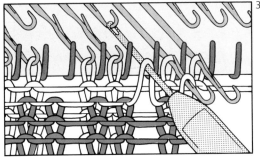

3.* Pick up the next loop – this is a longer loop formed where the needle was pushed back into non-working position – and place on to the next needle without a stitch. Pick up the next short loop: then, missing the next needle, place this loop on to the following needle. Repeat from * to end of row, placing the last loop on to the last needle. Change to main tension and continue knitting the pattern. The waste yarn can be removed either straight away or at the end of the piece of knitting.

TECHNICAL DATA

Hand-knit ribs

When hand-knitting ribs, cast on the required number of stitches using needles about two sizes smaller than those which are recommended for hand knitting on the yarn that you are using.

Work in rib for the correct depth, ending with a right-side row.

Bring forward the required number of needles to working position, then, with the wrong side of the rib facing and using the single transfer tool, hook each stitch individually on to the knitting machine needles, letting each one drop off the hand-knitting needle.

How to pick up dropped stitches

If a stitch is accidentally dropped, it can very quickly run down and form a ladder, especially if there are weights hanging on the knitting, but it is quite easily picked up again using the latch tool.

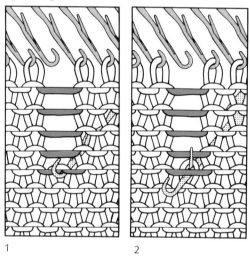

1   2

1. Insert the latch tool, from behind the knitting, into the stitch below the dropped stitch taking care not to split it.
2. Gently pull down on the knitting so that it unravels to the stitch to the hook.* Push the latch hook towards you through the fabric so that the stitch lies behind the latch and the latch is open, then catch the bar from the row above in the hook of the latch tool.

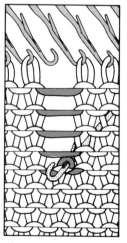

3   4

3. Pulling down gently on the fabric, draw the new stitch through.
4. Repeat from * until the final bar has been picked up, then, using the single transfer tool, hook the stitch back on to the empty needle and continue with the knitting.

Increasing and decreasing

In order to work shaping on a garment, for example, to increase the fabric along the side of the sleeve or to decrease the fabric at the neck or armhole, then increasing or decreasing needs to be worked. On both techniques, either a simple manoeuvre can be performed using a single transfer tool, or a method called fully fashioned shaping can be used. The choice is purely personal, although most patterns suggest which method to use. If the pattern just tells you to increase or decrease without specifying the method, then it is generally accepted that the simple method is to be used.

Simple increasing

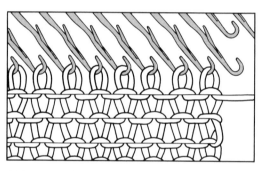

At the same end of the needlebed as the carriage, bring foward one needle to working position. Knit the row by passing the carriage across the needles. The empty needle will have caught the yarn as it passes across and formed a stitch.

Fully fashioned increasing

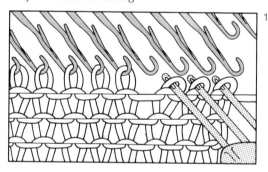

1. At either end of the needlebed and using the triple transfer tool, move the first three stitches one needle outwards. This leaves the fourth needle without a stitch.

TECHNICAL DATA

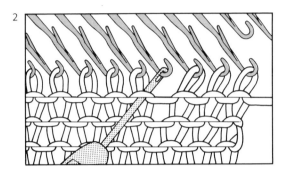

2. Insert the single transfer tool through the top of the stitch below the stitch on the fifth needle and place this loop on to the empty needle to prevent a hole forming when the row is knitted.

Simple decreasing

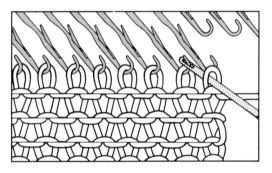

At either end of the needlebed, take the first stitch on to the single transfer tool and move it on to the second needle in. Push the empty needle back into non-working position.

Fully fashioned decreasing

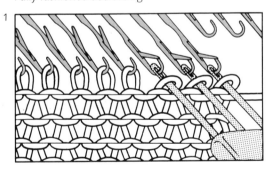

1. At either end of the needlebed, take the first three stitches on to the triple transfer tool, being careful not to drop one.

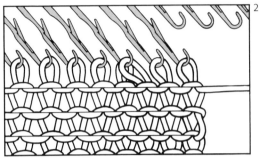

2. Move these three stitches one needle in, so that there are two stitches on the third needle. Push the empty needle back into non-working position.

Making up
Making up is just as important a part of making a garment as knitting it. Beautiful pieces of knitted fabric can be ruined by not taking enough time and trouble in sewing them together.

Once all the pieces have been knitted, it is essential that all loose ends, from joing in new balls of yarn or changing colour, are darned in securely and trimmed off. Do not cut the ends too short, or when the garment is worn the slightest movement will stretch the fabric and pull the ends out; then your garment could start to unravel.

Blocking and pressing
This is optional and purely a matter of personal preference. If you find it difficult to sew up the pieces when they are curling, then block and press the pieces. If you are at all unsure, and are afraid of damaging the fabric, test a sample swatch first or make up the pieces without blocking and pressing.

Blocking

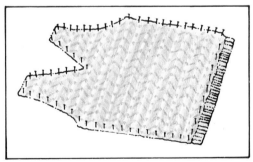

Place a thick layer of blanket on to a flat surface and cover with a smooth cloth. Lay out each piece of the garment, checking the measurements from the diagram, and pin out to size, leaving the ribbing unpinned.

If the yarn can be pressed, then either press the pieces under a damp cloth or steam them gently without placing any pressure on the fabric.

If the yarn cannot be pressed, place a damp cloth over the pinned-out fabric and leave until completely dry. Do not block or press ribbing.

TECHNICAL DATA

Finishing the neckband

For a really professional finish to a neckband, fold the neckband in half on to the right side of the garment and backstitch the open stitches into position, using the same colour yarn.

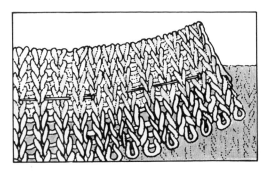

1. Fold the neckband in half on to the right side of the garment and pin into position.

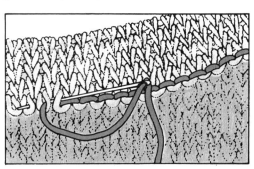

2. Thread a blunt-ended needle with matching yarn and join at beginning of neckband. Unravelling the waste yarn carefully as you work, backstitch through each individual stitch to the end of the neckband. Fasten off securely.

Joining the pieces

When sewing the pieces together, invisible stitch is the best stitch to use for sewing the straight seams because it is worked from the right side of the fabric and each stitch can be matched; this is very important if there are stripes or stitch patterns at the seams. For sewing curved seams, a backstitch seam is the strongest, and again it is not too difficult to match any necessary stripes or patterns.

Invisible stitch

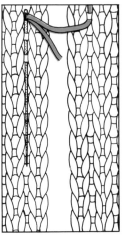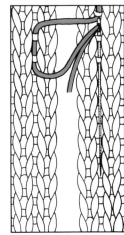

1. Place the two pieces to be joined side by side with the right sides facing up. Thread a blunt-ended needle with matching yarn and join at top of seam. Insert the needle under two horizontal threads, one stitch in, on the first piece.
2.* Draw the needle through, then pick up the corresponding two threads on the second piece.

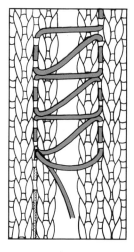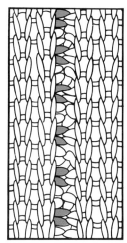

3. Draw the needle through, then return to the first piece and pick up the next two threads. Repeat from * several times more.
4. Gently pull the thread to close the seam. Repeat again from step 2 to the end of the seam, then fasten off securely.

TECHNICAL DATA

Backstitch seam

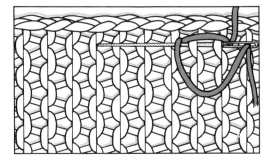

1. Place the two pieces to be joined with right sides together. Thread a blunt ended needle with matching yarn and join at beginning of seam.

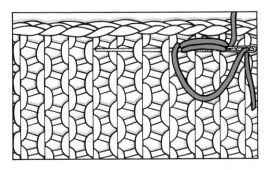

2. Insert the needle back through both thicknesses of fabric, a little to the right of the first stitch, then bring up the same distance to the left of the first stitch.

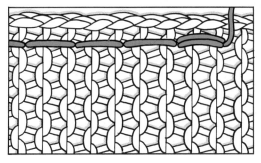

3.* Insert the needle back through the fabric where the stitch before last came out, then bring back out the same distance to the left of the last stitch. Repeat from * to the end of the seam, then fasten off securely.

Cables

Cables are easy to work on a knitting machine. To create the method most hand knitters use, with a purl stitch running down each side of the cable, it is necessary to have a double-bed machine or ribbing attachment. Cables worked in stocking stitch on a single bed machine can look equally effective.

When working a cable, you need to refer to the pattern to find out which needles to work the cable over and whether to use double or triple-transfer tools.

To make a cable

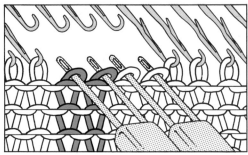

1. Knit to the position of the first cable twist.* Pick up the first set of stiches on to the first transfer tool and hold these in one hand; take the second transfer tool and place the second set of stitches on to it, and hold it in the other hand.

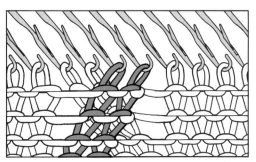

2. Cross the transfer tools left over right or right over left as given in the pattern, then place each set of stitches back on to the empty needles, thus changing the position of the stitches. Knit the required number of rows, then repeat from * for the number of times required.

YARN SUPPLIERS

For details of your nearest stockists of Rowan Yarns please write to:

UK
Rowan Yarns, Green Lane Mill, Holmfirth, West Yorkshire HD7 1RW, England.
Tel: (0484) 681881

Rowan Oxford,
102 Gloucester Green,
Oxford, Oxfordshire.
Tel: (0865) 793366

USA
The Westminster Trading Corporation,
5 Northern Boulevard, Amherst,
New Hampshire 03031,
United States of America.
Tel: (603) 886 5041

Cananda
Estelle Designs and Sales Ltd,
38 Continental Place,
Scarborough, Ontario,
Canada MIR 2T4.
Tel: (416) 298 9922

Denmark
Mosekonens Vaerksted,
Mosevej 13, L1 Binderup,
9600 Aars, Denmark.
Tel: (08) 656065

Norway
Eureka,
Kvakkestandgarden,
1400 Ski, Norway.
Tel: (0987) 1909

Holland
Beukers and Beukers,
DorpsStraat 9,
5327 Ar Hurwenen,
Holland.
Tel: (04182) 1764

West Germany
Textilwerkstatt,
Friedenstrasse 5,
3000 Hanover 1,
West Germany.
Tel: (0511) 818001

Australia
Sunspun Enterprises Pty Ltd,
191 Canterbury Road,
Canterbury 3126, Victoria,
Australia.
Tel: (03) 830 1609

New Zealand
Creative Fashion Centre,
PO Box 45083,
Epuni Railway, Lower Hutt,
New Zealand.
Tel: (04) 674 085

Sweden
Wincent,
Luntmakargatan 56,
113 58 Stockholm,
Sweden.
Tel: (08) 32 70 60

Japan
Diakeito Co Ltd,
1-5-23 Nakatsu Oyodo-Ku,
Osaka 531, Japan.
Tel: (06) 371 5653

Belgium
'Ma Campagne',
rue du village 4,
Septon 5482,
Durbuy, Belgium.
Tel: (86) 21 34 51

Italy
'La Compagnia Del Cotone',
Via Mazzini 44–10123,
Torino, Italy.
Tel: (011) 878381